PILLARS OF PROGRESS

ADB'S CONTRIBUTIONS TO THE SUSTAINABLE DEVELOPMENT GOALS

JULY 2024

ASIAN DEVELOPMENT BANK

ADB

6 ADB Avenue, Mandaluyong City, 1550 Metro Manila, Philippines
Tel +63 2 8632 4444; Fax +63 2 8636 2444
www.adb.org

ISBN 978-92-9270-804-7 (print); 978-92-9270-805-4 (electronic); 978-92-9270-806-1 (e-book)
Publication Stock No. SPR240361-2
DOI: http://dx.doi.org/10.22617/SPR240361-2

Corrigenda to ADB publications may be found at http://www.adb.org/publications/corrigenda.

Notes:
In this publication, "$" refers to United States dollars.
ADB recognizes "China" as the People's Republic of China.

Cover design by Karmen Karamanian and Charlene Claret.

Contents

Figures and Boxes

Figures

Boxes

Foreword

The 2030 Agenda for Sustainable Development serves as a globally agreed framework for action on the most pressing development challenges. At its halfway point, Asia and the Pacific is off track on all its targets. At the same time, with rapidly deepening threats to populations and the environment, the need to take stock and accelerate progress has never been more pressing.

President Masatsugu Asakawa
Asian Development Bank

This report reviews the contributions of the Asian Development Bank (ADB) to the Sustainable Development Goals (SDGs) and looks ahead to the work that still needs to be done. As the most populous and fastest-growing region in the world, Asia and the Pacific is critical for combating climate change and advancing the SDGs. ADB has been uniquely positioned to drive action to address these complex development challenges in the region. ADB has delivered by fostering cooperation between countries, bridging key development issues across sectors, and partnering with diverse stakeholders.

The halfway point to 2030 is an opportunity to address gaps, forge new partnerships, and catalyze regional cooperation. ADB's new operating model underscores our commitment to evolve by scaling up action and delivering high-quality, cross-sectoral solutions. Such solutions must also harness the private sector. Increased lending capacity and a decentralized decision-making approach under the new model and other recent reforms will ensure that ADB can mobilize resources, deploy staff skills, and share knowledge effectively.

Together, let us redouble our efforts and seize the opportunity to get back on track on the SDGs and achieve a prosperous, inclusive, resilient, and sustainable Asia and the Pacific.

The halfway point to 2030 is an opportunity to address gaps, forge new partnerships, and catalyze regional cooperation.

Abbreviations

ADB	–	Asian Development Bank
ADF	–	Asian Development Fund
ASEAN	–	Association of Southeast Asian Nations
COVID-19	–	coronavirus disease
CPS	–	country partnership strategy
CRF	–	corporate results framework
CSO	–	civil society organization
DMC	–	developing member country
ESCAP	–	Economic and Social Commission for Asia and the Pacific
FCAS	–	fragile and conflict-affected situations
GDP	–	gross domestic product
GHG	–	greenhouse gas
GRIS	–	green, resilient, inclusive, and sustainable
IMF	–	International Monetary Fund
Lao PDR	–	Lao People's Democratic Republic
LTC	–	long-term care
MDB	–	multilateral development bank
NDC	–	nationally determined contribution
OECD	–	Organisation for Economic Co-operation and Development
PRC	–	People's Republic of China
SDG	–	Sustainable Development Goal
SIDS	–	small island developing state
SMEs	–	small and medium-sized enterprises
UN	–	United Nations
UNDP	–	United Nations Development Programme
VNR	–	voluntary national review

Harvest season. An organic vegetable farmer in Boung Phao Village, Lao People's Democratic Republic, inspects her crops (photo by Ariel Javellana).

The blue hub. The ADB-supported Domestic Maritime Transport Project significantly increased efficiency and reduced congestion at Malé's domestic harbor in Maldives (photo by Ariel Javellana).

Introduction

As countries seek to achieve the Sustainable Development Goals (SDGs), multilateral institutions like the Asian Development Bank (ADB) play a crucial role and are uniquely positioned to mobilize the resources, expertise, and partnerships needed to drive progress.

At the halfway point to 2030, and against the backdrop of multiple crises stalling progress, this report is a timely reflection on ADB's impactful contributions since the SDGs were adopted by United Nations (UN) member states in 2015. With a focus on the thematic clusters of the SDGs—people, planet, prosperity, sustainable infrastructure—as well as the critical crosscutting themes of mobilizing finance and driving knowledge, the report showcases ADB's internal alignment with the 2030 Agenda for Sustainable Development and the many ways in which it supports its members in implementing and making progress toward the SDGs. The report shines a light on diverse projects and initiatives that have positively contributed to improved development prospects, while also identifying areas that can drive systemic solutions and accelerated progress across the region.

In March 2021, at the start of the "Decade of Action" to meet the SDGs and ADB's Strategy 2030, ADB published its inaugural SDGs report entitled *ADB's Support for the Sustainable Development Goals: Enabling the 2030 Agenda for Sustainable Development through Strategy 2030.*[1] The report marked an important milestone as the first comprehensive outline of ADB's approach toward advancing the SDGs in Asia and the Pacific.

The first report laid the foundation for this new publication, which continues to reaffirm ADB's deep commitment to the SDGs and aims to evaluate ADB's efforts, inform future planning, and promote collaboration.

1 ADB. 2021. *ADB's Support for the Sustainable Development Goals: Enabling the 2030 Agenda for Sustainable Development through Strategy 2030.*

I. SDG Progress and Implementation in Asia and the Pacific

Overview of SDG Progress in Asia and the Pacific

The SDGs, adopted by world leaders in 2015, signaled a historic achievement: a shared commitment by all 193 UN member states to end poverty, while protecting the planet, by 2030.

At the halfway point toward 2030, the ambitious agenda for addressing global development challenges has been challenged by unprecedented shocks in geopolitics, energy and economics, as well as a pandemic, and the growing impacts of the climate crisis, which have slowed progress toward several SDGs.

To date, progress across Asia and the Pacific falls short of the halfway mark, and progress varied for each of the goals and within developing member countries (DMCs). As the SDGs cover a broad range of issues, there is no clear success story on one SDG or country. What is clear, however, is that some progress has been made in all SDGs except two where reversals have taken place: SDG 13 (climate action) and SDG 14 (life below water). Figure 1 summarizes the collective progress on each SDG of ADB DMCs.

Living conditions in Asia and the Pacific have transformed in the past 60 years. Poverty in the region has fallen at a staggering pace. In 1981, four out of five people in Asia and the Pacific lived in poverty. By 2022, fewer than four in 100 people, or 3.9%, were considered poor. However, in 2022, due to the coronavirus disease (COVID-19) pandemic and the cost-of-living crisis, ADB estimates that around 78 million people were pushed back into poverty. It will take time for this shock in poverty to reverse. By 2030, around 1.26 billion people in Asia and the Pacific are projected to be economically vulnerable.[2]

Climate change impacts continue to increase with temperatures edging up as greenhouse gas (GHG) emissions continue to rise due to unsustainable consumption and production patterns. This further exacerbates the adverse impacts on vulnerable communities who have historically contributed the least to climate change.[3] This extends to biodiversity loss, in water and on land, that undermines employment and food systems in the region, especially in least developed countries, which lack coping capacity and are more exposed to hazards. Over the next decades and beyond, inland fisheries in large river basins in Asia are projected to be at great risk due to an increase in water temperature, majorly affecting the Ganges, Krishna, and Mekong rivers.[4] These trends drive the continued regression on SDG 13 (climate action) and amplify the vulnerabilities captured by SDG 14 (life below water) despite increased climate policy reforms across the region.

The economies of the region have been recovering at an uneven pace. Unemployment has started to fall amid a surge of demand for services and tourism following the loosening of COVID-19-related travel restrictions. In most countries, trade deficits are still high, in some cases exceeding the equivalent of more than one-half of their gross domestic product (GDP).

At the halfway point toward 2030, the ambitious agenda for addressing global development challenges has been challenged by unprecedented shocks.

---

2 ADB. 2023. *Key Indicators for Asia and the Pacific 2023.*

3 Intergovernmental Panel on Climate Change. 2023. *Climate Change 2023: Synthesis Report. Contribution of Working Groups I, II and III to the Sixth Assessment Report of the Intergovernmental Panel on Climate Change.* pp. 35–115.

4 UN, ADB, and United Nations Development Programme (UNDP). 2023. *People and Planet: Addressing the Interlinked Challenges of Climate Change, Poverty and Hunger in Asia and the Pacific.*

Figure 1: SDG Progress in ADB Developing Member Countries

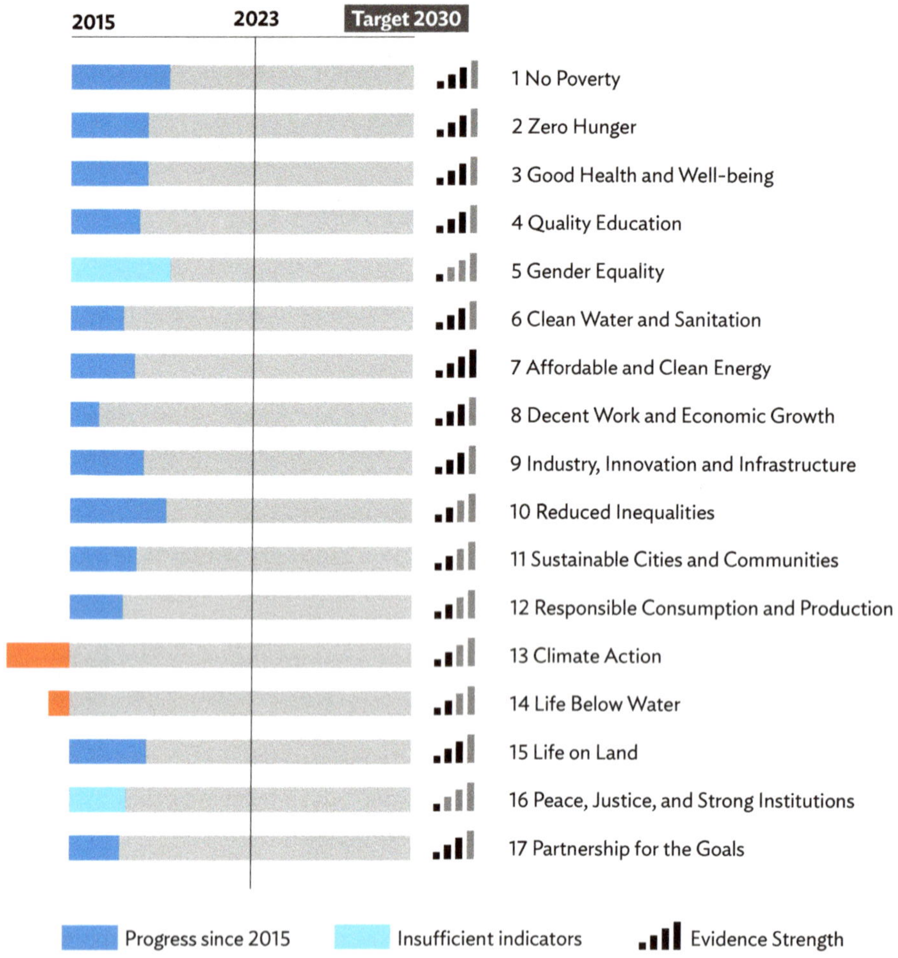

SDG = Sustainable Development Goal.

Note: Data availability varies between countries and is still lacking for many SDG indicators. However, the Economic and Social Commission for Asia and the Pacific estimates that the number of indicators with sufficient data doubled, from 63 in 2017 to 128 in 2022. "Insufficient Indicators" means that there are too few indicators with sufficient data to ensure the robustness of the progress shown.

Source: Asia–Pacific SDG Partnership Data Portal. 2024.

Status of SDG Implementation in Asia and the Pacific

Since 2015, most countries in Asia and the Pacific have taken steps to implement the 2030 Agenda at the national level, by creating an institutional architecture and frameworks for SDG implementation, aligning national development plans and policies with the SDGs, incorporating planning, monitoring systems, and establishing financing mechanisms. Additionally, some countries have taken measures to implement the SDGs at the subnational level, with added challenges where local governments lack the expertise and resources to do so.

Progress is reviewed globally through the High-Level Political Forum on Sustainable Development (HLPF), the UN's main forum for addressing the global sustainable development agenda. The process is centered on countries presenting a voluntary national review (VNR) of their progress in implementing the SDGs. By the end of 2023, 38 of ADB's DMCs had submitted VNRs to the UN forum, 30 of them more than once. The Asia–Pacific Forum on Sustainable Development, an annual intergovernmental forum, informed by subregional consultations on selected themes, reviews progress on the 2030 Agenda and SDGs regionally.

The extent to which countries in Asia and the Pacific have implemented the SDGs varies. Most countries have taken steps to integrate the SDGs into their national development plans. Some 39 of ADB's DMCs have established intragovernmental or multistakeholder coordination mechanisms to support the agenda. Over 33 countries are integrating SDG targets and indicators in their development plans to some extent. Eighteen DMCs have passed a law or issued a decree in relation to the SDGs. Figure 2 summarizes the measures DMCs have taken to implement the SDGs since 2015.

Figure 2: SDG Implementation Status in Asia and the Pacific (2016–2024)

38 DMCs HAVE CONDUCTED VOLUNTARY NATIONAL REVIEWS
OF WHICH 30 DMCs HAVE CONDUCTED VOLUNTARY NATIONAL REVIEWS TWICE
AT LEAST 18 DMCs HAVE SDG-RELATED DECREES OR LAWS
39 DMCs HAVE SDG COORDINATION MECHANISMS
MORE THAN 33 DMCs ARE INTEGRATING SDG TARGETS AND INDICATORS IN DEVELOPMENT PLANS
= DMC.

ADB = Asian Development Bank, DMC = developing member country, SDG = Sustainable Development Goal.

Source: Asian Development Bank.

II. ADB's Approach in Support of the SDGs

Overview of ADB's Approach

ADB's vision is a prosperous, inclusive, resilient, and sustainable Asia and the Pacific, which reflects the aspirations of the 2030 Agenda for Sustainable Development. Since the adoption of the SDGs in 2015, ADB has been committed to supporting its DMCs to make progress on attaining the SDGs and has made significant contributions to the region's sustainable development.

ADB participated in the first UN SDG Summit in New York in 2015 where it applauded the increased ambition of the SDGs and stated that it "stands ready to provide tailored support to respond to specific challenges regionally, nationally, and locally."[5] Since then, ADB has been working with its DMCs to deliver the SDGs through four critical areas of support: (i) strategic alignment of its operations to the SDGs; (ii) direct financing of member countries and the private sector in support of the SDGs; (iii) mobilizing additional finance for the SDGs from a wide range of sources; and (iv) providing knowledge, data, and policy dialogue on SDG progress and implementation (Figure 3). Within these areas of support, ADB uses technology and partnerships to drive initiatives that accelerate progress.

Figure 3: How ADB Supports the SDGs in Asia and the Pacific

DMC = developing member country, SDG = Sustainable Development Goal.

Source: Asian Development Bank.

5 ADB's Statement at the UN Sustainable Development Summit. ADB Vice-President (Operations 2) Stephen P. Groff. 27 September 2015.

Through the activities in these four areas, ADB aims to increase implementation and achievement of the SDGs in DMCs, and contribute to realizing its vision for a prosperous, inclusive, resilient and sustainable Asia and the Pacific. In doing so, ADB is channeling increased financing toward supporting the SDGs, improving the integration of the SDGs into national and subnational development planning, strengthening DMCs' SDG institutional architecture, and enhancing the knowledge and data on topics related to the SDGs. Figure 4 outlines ADB's Theory of Change in support of the SDGs in the region and sets out the activities and outputs that are integral to the process. The next sections of the report will describe these activities in detail and highlight a broad range of examples of ADB's support for the SDGs.

Figure 4: Theory of Change to Drive SDG Attainment in Asia and the Pacific

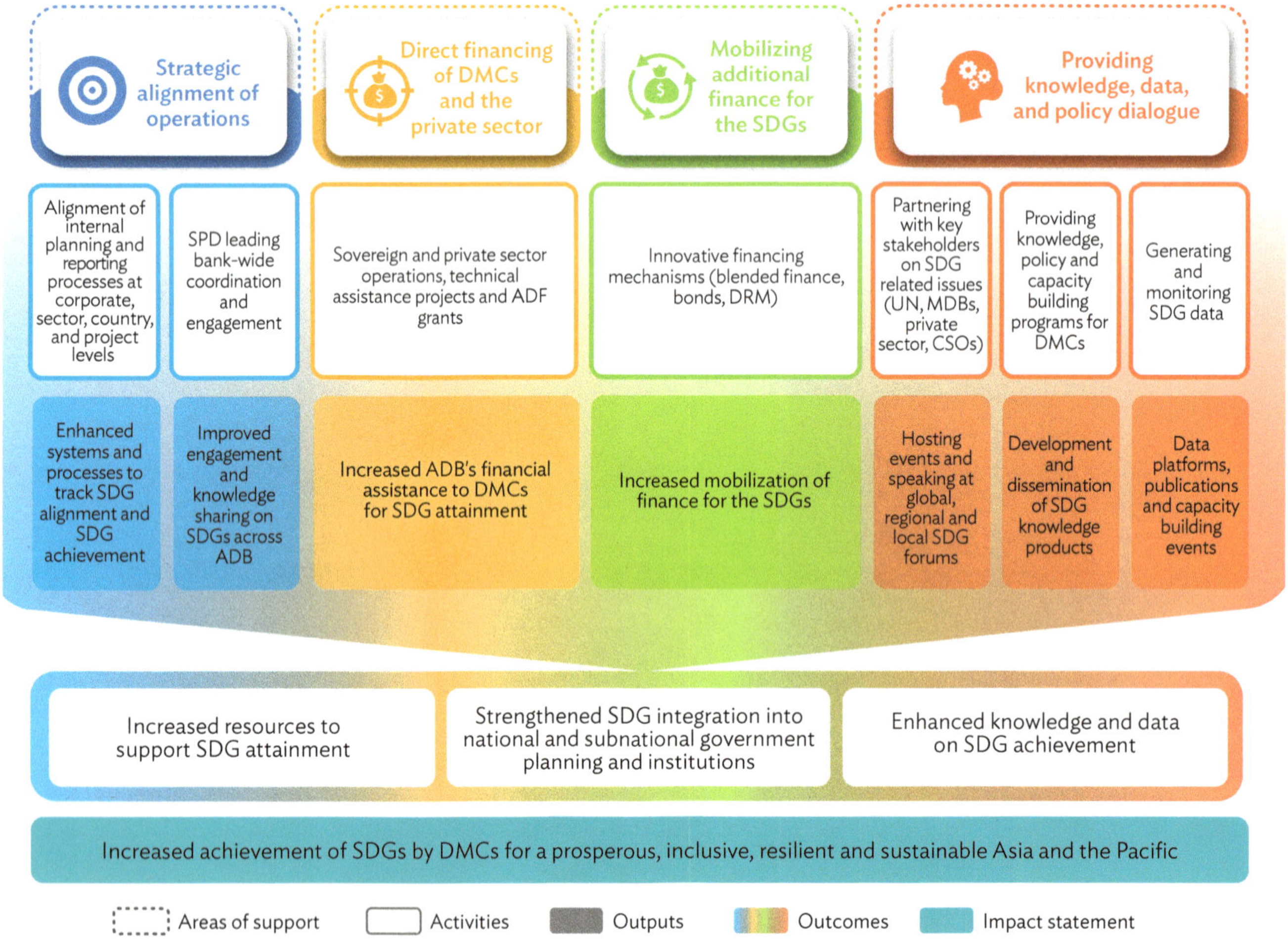

ADB = Asian Development Bank; ADF = Asian Development Fund; CSO = civil society organization; DMC = developing member country; DRM = disaster risk management; MDB = multilateral development bank; SDG = Sustainable Development Goal; SPD = Strategy, Policy, and Partnerships Department; UN = United Nations.

Source: Asian Development Bank.

Strategic Alignment of ADB's Operations to the SDGs

Since the 2030 Agenda was adopted, ADB has taken several steps to embed the SDGs in its strategies, planning, and reporting processes at all levels of the organization (namely at corporate, country, and project levels).

Corporate alignment. At a corporate level, ADB's seven operational priorities set out in the Strategy 2030 are mapped to the SDGs, and its operations are designed to help meet these goals and their targets.[6] Figure 5 visualizes how each of the operational priorities aligns with the SDGs and identifies the crosscutting goals targeted across all of them.

ADB's corporate results framework (CRF) provides the basis for reporting on ADB's strategic, operational, and organizational performance, and facilitates learning and performance improvement.[7] The current 2019-2024 framework has four levels: Level 1 tracks development progress in Asia and the Pacific with indicators that are either SDG indicators or directly aligned with SDG indicators. Level 2 assesses results from ADB's completed operations; Level 3 captures ADB's operational management; and Level 4 captures

Figure 5: ADB's Strategy 2030 Operational Priorities Alignment with the SDGs

ADB = Asian Development Bank, SDG = Sustainable Development Goal, OP = Operational Prioritiy.

Source: Asian Development Bank.

6 ADB. 2018. *Strategy 2030: Achieving a Prosperous, Inclusive, Resilient And Sustainable Asia and the Pacific.*

7 ADB. *Development Effectiveness Review.* (17 years: 2007–2023).

ADB's organizational effectiveness—all with indicators that are largely aligned with, or derived from, official SDG indicators. Figure 6 shows how ADB's CRF aligns with the SDGs, targets, and indicators. This framework is currently being updated and will be replaced by the new 2025-2030 CRF.

Country-level alignment. The alignment of ADB's country engagement with the SDGs is reflected in the bank's country partnership strategies (CPSs) with each DMC, which serve as the primary planning instrument that guides ADB's country-level operations. As an input to the CPS development process, SDG implementation synthesis notes are prepared to provide specific country context on the SDG agenda, covering information on the country's SDG architecture, implementation, and progress, and helping identify needs. Each CPS also contains a results framework that monitors and tracks how ADB-supported programming will help achieve development outcomes, in alignment with the SDGs as well as the country's national and global development objectives.

Project-level alignment. The SDGs are integrated into ADB's electronic project classification system (referred to as eOperations) and are reflected in the project-at-a-glance summary of reports and recommendations of the President for new projects. This allows the SDGs to be considered at the project design phase, providing a clear mapping of contributions to Strategy 2030, reported annually in ADB's Development Effectiveness Review. The system is assessed and updated regularly to ensure that projects are classified in a way that makes clear which SDGs they support. Figure 7 shows how ADB's portfolio in 2023 is mapped to the SDGs using data from the project classification system. Each project is linked to at least one sector-related SDG and a few crosscutting SDGs.

Figure 6: ADB Corporate Results Framework Alignment with SDGs (2019–2024)

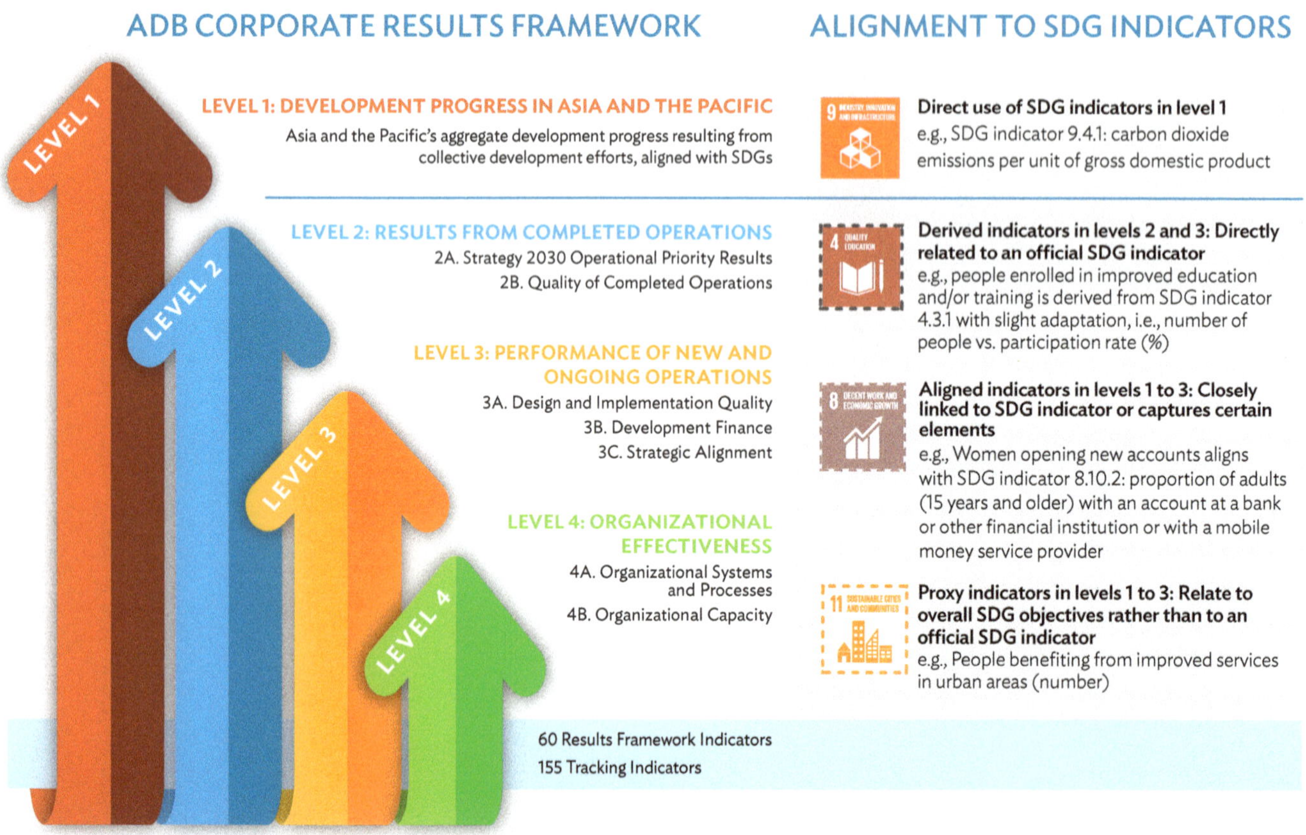

ADB CORPORATE RESULTS FRAMEWORK
ALIGNMENT TO SDG INDICATORS
LEVEL 1
LEVEL 2
LEVEL 3
LEVEL 4
LEVEL 1: DEVELOPMENT PROGRESS IN ASIA AND THE PACIFIC
Asia and the Pacific's aggregate development progress resulting from collective development efforts, aligned with SDGs
LEVEL 2: RESULTS FROM COMPLETED OPERATIONS
2A. Strategy 2030 Operational Priority Results
2B. Quality of Completed Operations
LEVEL 3: PERFORMANCE OF NEW AND ONGOING OPERATIONS
3A. Design and Implementation Quality
3B. Development Finance
3C. Strategic Alignment
LEVEL 4: ORGANIZATIONAL EFFECTIVENESS
4A. Organizational Systems and Processes
4B. Organizational Capacity
60 Results Framework Indicators
155 Tracking Indicators
Direct use of SDG indicators in level 1
e.g., SDG indicator 9.4.1: carbon dioxide emissions per unit of gross domestic product
Derived indicators in levels 2 and 3: Directly related to an official SDG indicator
e.g., people enrolled in improved education and/or training is derived from SDG indicator 4.3.1 with slight adaptation, i.e., number of people vs. participation rate (%)
Aligned indicators in levels 1 to 3: Closely linked to SDG indicator or captures certain elements
e.g., Women opening new accounts aligns with SDG indicator 8.10.2: proportion of adults (15 years and older) with an account at a bank or other financial institution or with a mobile money service provider
Proxy indicators in levels 1 to 3: Relate to overall SDG objectives rather than to an official SDG indicator
e.g., People benefiting from improved services in urban areas (number)

ADB = Asian Development Bank, SDG = Sustainable Development Goal.

Source: Asian Development Bank.

Figure 7: SDGs Supported by ADB Projects in 2023

ADB = Asian Development Bank, SDG = Sustainable Development Goal.

Source: Asian Development Bank.

Additionally, ADB, through its Private Sector Operations Department (PSOD), uses the Harmonized Indicators for Private Sector Operations (HIPSO) to report the interim results of the contributions to the SDGs of its active portfolio in its Development Effectiveness Report.[8] To do so, PSOD aggregates its SDG results through data obtained from clients' annual or biannual development effectiveness monitoring reports, which clients submit as part of the project performance monitoring process.

Recent Reforms to Strengthen Support

Responding to a rapidly evolving development landscape in Asia and the Pacific, ADB is undertaking a **Midterm Review of its Strategy 2030 (S2030 MTR)**. The S2030 MTR outlines how ADB is responding to the global multilateral development bank (MDB) evolution agenda of strengthening and upgrading development banks to address new challenges. It anchors and links ADB's various corporate transformation initiatives, focusing particularly on support for global and regional public goods, reflecting new development challenges as corporate priorities, and updating finances, people, and internal systems and processes to achieve greater impact. In this vein, the current **CRF** is also being reviewed to realign the corporate performance indicators for 2025-2030 and take account of S2030 MTR.

To serve the changing needs of its DMCs more effectively, in 2023, ADB launched a **New Operating Model** to increase its capacity as Asia and the Pacific's climate bank; spur private sector engagement and investment; provide a wide range of integrated and innovative development solutions; and modernize how ADB works. These four shifts, together with an ongoing decentralization process that will strengthen country offices and empower decision-making closer to clients, will lead to more innovative solutions and greater mobilization of finance for ADB members to reignite progress toward the SDGs (Figure 8).

ADB, a front-runner in supporting MDB Evolution, in 2023 announced capital management reforms to unlock $100 billion in new funding over the next decade and support Asia and the Pacific to meet the SDGs. The reforms were introduced through an update of **ADB's Capital Adequacy Framework** to expand annual new

8 ADB. *Development Effectiveness Reports: Private Sector Operations.* Manila.

Figure 8: How ADB's New Operating Model Shifts Will Drive Accelerated SDG Progress

CLIMATE CHANGE
By increasing its capacity as Asia and the Pacific's climate bank, ADB will drive the regional leadership needed for a collective response to climate change and ensure that climate action linkages with other SDGs are addressed.
PRIVATE SECTOR DEVELOPMENT
ADB's strengthened role as a catalyst for the private sector will support wider mobilization of finance for the SDGs.
SOLUTIONS
By working across sectors, with one window for sovereign and private sector operations, ADB will provide the integrated solutions and development impact that the SDGs require.
WAYS OF WORKING
By moving closer to clients and improving agility in operations, ADB will more effectively address its developing member countries' SDG needs.

ADB = Asian Development Bank, SDG = Sustainable Development Goal.

Source: Asian Development Bank.

commitments capacity to more than $36 billion —an increase of around $10 billion, or about 40%. The measures, which will enable ADB to provide up to $360 billion of its own financing to its DMCs and private sector clients over the next decade, are designed to ensure ADB maintains its AAA credit rating and its ability to provide DMCs with funding at low cost and with long maturities. The reforms further safeguard ADB's AAA credit rating through the introduction of a recovery plan that would prevent capital erosion during periods of financial stress.

In 2024, ADB announced the $5 billion replenishment for the **Asian Development Fund (ADF)** 14, the largest-ever commitment to ADB's grant operations, which aims to transform life in the poorest and most vulnerable DMCs in Asia and the Pacific. ADF 14 focuses on climate change adaptation, disaster risk reduction, promoting gender equality, and driving forward regional cooperation and integration. Box 1 provides an overview of these three key dimensions of the MDB Evolution at ADB.

Biodiversity conservation. Located in the middle section of the northern foothill of the Qinling mountains in Shaanxi Province in the People's Republic of China (PRC), the ADB-supported Qinling National Botanical Garden is the first national-level botanical garden in the PRC (photo by Deng Jia).

Box 1: Multilateral Development Banks Evolution at ADB

There has been a global call for reforms to multilateral development banks (MDBs) to work as a system to address mounting challenges, in what has been referred to as the "MDB Evolution," a road map for "bigger, better, and bolder" MDBs. There are three key dimensions of how Asian Development Bank (ADB) is stepping up to tackle the MDB Evolution internally (Figure):

1. **Mission and Vision:** Responding to a rapidly evolving development landscape and heightened Sustainable Development Goal (SDG) challenges in Asia and the Pacific, ADB is working on the **Midterm Review of its Strategy 2030,** which is elevating the importance of development that explicitly targets transborder benefits and delivery of global and regional public goods. The **Climate Change Action Plan 2023–2030** is an important driver to strengthen ADB's position as Asia and the Pacific's climate bank.

2. **Operational Approaches:** ADB has introduced a **New Operating Model** to make the bank fit for purposes given the region's changing development challenges. The new model is more client-centric, with new ways of working across sectors and closer to clients, allowing for a wider range of high-quality development solutions. It elevates ADB's role as the region's climate bank and strengthens its work to develop the private sector and mobilize larger amounts of finance. An update of ADB's results management system with the **new Corporate Results Framework 2025–2030** will better reflect the key development priorities of the region.

3. **Financial Model and Capacity:** ADB's **Capital Adequacy Framework Review** responds to the need for increased finance to be directed toward the SDGs and is articulated through an extra $100 billion in funding over the next decade. The $5 billion **14th replenishment of the Asian Development Fund 2025–2028**, the largest ever commitment to grant operations, also drives the transformation agenda with increased capacity to support the poorest and most vulnerable countries.

Figure: The Three Dimensions of the Multilateral Development Bank Evolution at ADB

ADB = Asian Development Bank, ADF = Asian Development Fund.

Source: Asian Development Bank.

Source: Asian Development Bank.

Collaboration with Development Partners

Through **partnering with the UN system**, ADB ensures its work on supporting its DMCs is fully integrated into the regional and global policy processes of the 2030 Agenda. The report highlights different partnerships and engagements with several UN agencies supporting the SDGs. An outstanding example of collaboration is the Asia–Pacific SDG Partnership which provides knowledge, policy dialogue, and data for advancing the SDGs in the region (Box 10).

ADB is part of the CFO Coalition for the SDGs, the world's largest corporate sustainability initiative launched by the UN Global Compact. It is a nonbinding pact, where global chief financial officers and other executives can collaborate with peers, investors, financial institutions, and UN agencies to develop principles, frameworks, and recommendations to integrate the SDGs into corporate finance and create a market to mainstream SDG investments.

ADB has been **working closely with other MDBs**, through the MDB Working Group on Managing for Development Results (MfDR), to support common approaches to reporting on contributions to the SDGs. In 2020, 11 MDBs and the International Monetary Fund (IMF) published the report *Financing the Sustainable Development Goals: The Contributions of the Multilateral Development Banks*[9] which outlines the steps the 12 institutions are taking to support the SDGs. The SDGs workstream of the MDB working group for MfDR has benchmarked the different approaches undertaken by MDBs to align projects with the SDGs "ex ante," that is at project design phase, and to develop principles for harmonizing this alignment.

ADB has been **cooperating with the Organisation for Economic Co-operation and Development (OECD)** for many years through different initiatives that aim to promote development effectiveness and support the attainment of the SDGs through effective results measurement and management. Data from ADB's SDG tagging project system is shared with the OECD for the Total Official Support for Sustainable Development (TOSSD), an international standard for measuring the full array of resources to promote sustainable development in developing countries. The TOSSD is supported by a large, diverse group of countries and multilateral organizations committed to tracking SDG-related investments in an open, inclusive, and transparent manner.

ADB cooperates with a broad range of **civil society organizations (CSOs)** on a project basis to strengthen its efforts to reduce poverty and increase the effectiveness, quality, and sustainability of its operations. Some of these collaborations are reflected in this report within the project highlights by SDG.

ADB also partners with **universities, private sector entities, and networks**, to advance support toward the SDGs in Asia and the Pacific.

Timeline of Key Milestones

Since the adoption of the 2030 Agenda in 2015, ADB has embarked on a journey, aligning its internal processes and strategic initiatives with the SDGs, delivering projects and programs in support of the SDGs, and participating in regional and global policy processes. Figure 9 presents a timeline of the key milestones in ADB's journey of supporting the 2030 Agenda and aligning its internal processes to the SDGs.

---

9 11 MDBs and IMF. 2020. *Financing the Sustainable Development Goals. The Contributions of the Multilateral Development Banks.*

Figure 9: Timeline of Key Milestones of ADB's Alignment and Engagement with the SDGs

ADB = Asian Development Bank; ADF = Asian Development Fund; APFSD = Asia–Pacific Forum on Sustainable Development; CFO = chief financial officer; CPS = country partnership strategy; CRF = corporate results framework; ESCAP = Economic and Social Commission for Asia and the Pacific; HIPSO = Harmonized Indicators for Private Sector Operations; HLPF = High-Level Political Forum on Sustainable Development; MDB = multilateral development bank; OCR = ordinary capital resources; PCS = project classification system; SDG = Sustainable Development Goal; SPD = Strategy, Policy, and Partnerships Department; SPRA = Results Management and Aid Effectiveness Division; UNDP = United Nations Development Programme; UNGA = United Nations General Assembly.

Source: Asian Development Bank.

III. ADB's Support for the SDGs

Overview

ADB's portfolio has been responsive to the changing development challenges and needs in the region. This is evidenced by the varying share of supported SDGs each year (Figure 10). In 2020, for example, the share of ADB projects in health (SDG 3) surged amid the COVID-19 pandemic. From 2021, ADB also increased focus on water (SDG 6) and urban infrastructure (SDG 11) projects to support cities at the forefront of efforts to contain the COVID-19 pandemic. More recently, with the onset of a global poly-crisis with far-reaching consequences for energy and food systems, there has been an increase in projects that support food security (SDG 2) and clean and affordable energy (SDG 7). Support directed toward SDG 14 (life below water) has emerged in recent years amid ADB's healthy oceans initiative, thus demonstrating support for a goal that has been regressing.

Over the years, support has been strong and consistent for SDG 1 (no poverty), SDG 5 (gender equality), SDG 10 (reduced inequalities), and SDG 13 (climate action), reflecting the priority areas of ADB's strategy, and the crosscutting thematic nature of these SDGs. Notably, there has been an uptick in support to SDG 13 (climate action) and SDG 17 (partnership for the goals), which reflects ADB's stronger focus on climate and mobilizing private sector capital for sustainable development.

Since 2016 ADB has provided $183.5 billion to sustainable development in Asia and the Pacific and mobilized $107.8 billion in cofinancing. Of the first figure, $42.1 billion has focused on climate-related and $11.9 billion on social protection projects.

Figure 10: SDGs Supported by ADB Project Portfolio (2019–2023)

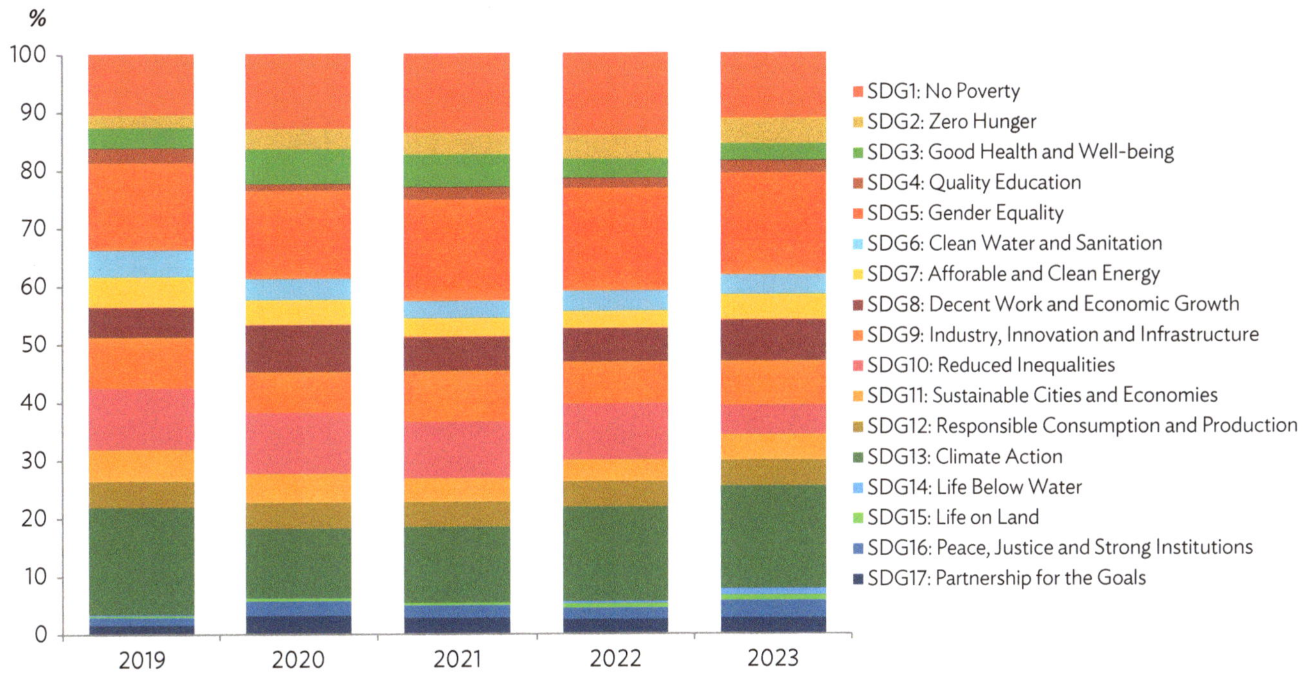

ADB = Asian Development Bank, SDG = Sustainable Development Goal.

Note: 2016 to 2018 are not included due to insufficient data.

Source: Asian Development Bank.

Highlights of ADB's Contributions by SDG Cluster

Most of ADB's projects and programs support several SDGs and many of them address multiple, interconnected issues, or "nexus challenges." The following section highlights ADB's key contributions to the 2030 Agenda. It is organized around four interlinked SDG clusters: people, planet, prosperity, and sustainable infrastructure, and their associated SDGs (Figure 11).

SDG 17, which is about revitalizing the global partnership for sustainable development (and issues relating to mobilizing finance and driving knowledge for the SDGs specifically), is addressed in a separate chapter.

Each cluster provides an overview of progress toward the SDGs in the region, ADB's overall approach and results, and examples of selected initiatives. Crosscutting initiatives that specifically address the interlinked nature of the SDGs and propose solutions at their nexus are highlighted in boxes.

Within each SDG, the report highlights a number of initiatives and projects at different stages of implementation, that have been selected to reflect the breadth and depth of ADB's support to the 2030 Agenda. Some of the projects highlighted have already closed and their results are reported; for more recent or ongoing projects, the intended outcomes are indicated.

Figure 11: SDG Clusters

SDG = Sustainable Development Goal.

Source: Asian Development Bank.

Most of ADB's projects and programs support several SDGs and many of them address multiple, interconnected issues, or "nexus challenges."

Regional progress

Asia and the Pacific is home to 4.6 billion people or 60% of the global population.[10] This means that the region's trajectory has a tremendous impact on sustainable development at the global level. Despite significant efforts to enhance food security in recent years, around 396 million people in the region remain undernourished, and over a billion people were still affected by moderate to severe food insecurity in 2021.[11] Similarly, Asia and the Pacific has witnessed a profound transformation in terms of various health outcomes, especially in sexual, reproductive, maternal, newborn, child, and adolescent health, along with progress in tackling certain communicable diseases. However, in many countries, socioeconomic inequality, structural discrimination, and gender norms remain barriers to universal access to health care.[12]

Significant progress has also been made in the region to improve the accessibility and quality of education. This has involved, among others, narrowing or eliminating gender disparities in opportunities and securing equitable access to all levels of education and vocational training for vulnerable groups.[13] Despite progress in some areas, gender disparities persist, particularly when it comes to women's economic opportunities and voice and influence in society. Over the 3 decades, the region is expected to continue to urbanize, with the urban population projected to rise from 56% in 2021 to 68% by 2050.[14]

Key features of ADB's approach

The SDGs that focus on people are central to ADB's strategy, with three of its seven operational priorities centered around these goals. ADB's Operational Priority 1 aims to address remaining poverty and reduce inequalities by enhancing human capital, social protection, and quality jobs. Operational Priority 2 promotes gender equality, through a strong focus on women's empowerment and by mainstreaming gender equality on ADB's operations—with a target of at least 75% of ADB's committed sovereign and nonsovereign operations supporting gender equality by 2030. In 2022, this target was surpassed and 99% (using a three-year average) of committed operations promoted gender equality.[15] ADB's Operational Priority 4 promotes the need for integrated solutions to realize green, competitive, resilient, and inclusive cities that address the social dimensions of urbanization, such as human-centered design, and the needs of women, older people, people with disabilities, and migrants.

10 UNFPA Asia and the Pacific. Population Trends.
11 FAO, UNICEF, WFP, and WHO. 2023. *Asia and the Pacific – Regional Overview of Food Security and Nutrition 2022: Urban Food Security and Nutrition*. Bangkok.
12 ESCAP. 2021. *SDG 3: Good Health and Well-Being*. Bangkok.
13 ESCAP. 2022. *SDG 4: Quality Education*. Bangkok.
14 UN-Habitat. 2022. *World Cities Report 2022: Envisaging the Future of Cities*. Nairobi.
15 The figure takes into account operation commitments classified as gender equity, effective gender mainstreaming, and some gender elements.

ADB's Impact

(accumulated results from completed operations in 2016–2023)

2 ZERO HUNGER

- 465.3 million people benefiting from increased rural investment
- 166,000 farmers using quality farm inputs and sustainable mechanization[a]
- 3.12 million hectares of land with higher productivity[a]

3 GOOD HEALTH AND WELL-BEING

- 435.8 million people benefiting from improved health, education, and social protection
- 158.9 million poor and vulnerable people with improved standards of living

4 QUALITY EDUCATION

- 21.9 million people enrolled in improved education and/or training
- 10 million women and girls completing secondary and tertiary education, and/or other training

5 GENDER EQUALITY

- 12.5 million women and girls with increased time savings, who spend less time on unpaid household or care work[a]
- 18.5 million women and girls with increased resilience to climate change, disasters, and other external shocks[a]

11 SUSTAINABLE CITIES AND COMMUNITIES

- 153.8 million people benefiting from improved services in urban areas
- 119,000 urban infrastructure assets established or improved[a]

[a] Figure does not include data from 2016 to 2018 as indicator was introduced in ADB's corporate results framework 2019-2024.

Source: ADB's Development Effectiveness Review.

Bird's-eye view. Urban landscape of Yerevan, Armenia (photo by Eric Sales).

Highlights of ADB projects

2 ZERO HUNGER

Food insecurity is threatening to reverse decades of development progress in Asia and the Pacific. ADB's support for SDG 2 ranges from regional large-scale systemic investment programs and initiatives to country-level project investments that strengthen the resilience and efficiency of food and agricultural value chains. In recent years, ADB has been incorporating climate aspects into its food security programs addressing the important interlinkages between SDG 2 and SDG 13.

In September 2022, ADB announced plans to provide $14 billion in financing over 2022–2025 in a comprehensive program to ease the food crisis in the region and improve long-term food security by strengthening food systems against the impacts of climate change and biodiversity loss.[16] This expands ADB's already significant support for food security in the region, where nearly 1.1 billion people lack healthy diets due to poverty and elevated food prices.[17]

Natural capital approaches offer a range of innovative tools that consider the value of the natural environment for people and the economy. In November 2023, ADB and the Global Environment Facility, a multilateral funding program, launched the Natural Capital Fund, a $15 million concessional fund aimed at enhancing food security while protecting and restoring natural capital in ADB's DMCs.

There are many examples of country-level financial support for food security. In Indonesia, many farming communities struggle to access water. Oftentimes, this results in poor harvests and low incomes for farmers. In May 2017, ADB committed $500 million to support Indonesia's Irrigation Improvement Program, including cofinancing from the Association of Southeast Asian Nations (ASEAN) Infrastructure Fund ($100 million) and the World Bank ($28 million). The financing package supported the delivery of sustainable and more productive irrigated agriculture in 74 districts. About 4,500 water user associations, 88 irrigation commissions, and other agencies are now better equipped to jointly manage their water resources. As of 2023, the program had helped rehabilitate irrigation schemes covering around 523,000 hectares.

ADB has been incorporating climate aspects into its food security programs addressing the important nexus between SDG 2 and SDG 13.

Box 2: Greater Mekong Subregion Sustainable Agriculture and Food Security Program

Agriculture remains an important economic pillar in the countries of the Greater Mekong Subregion (GMS). More than 70% of the subregion's rural population directly depends on the sector for their livelihoods, with women playing a vital role as farmers, agricultural laborers, or entrepreneurs. However, underdeveloped infrastructure and poor capacity are major barriers within the subregion's agricultural value chains.

Through the Greater Mekong Subregion Sustainable Agriculture and Food Security Program, the Asian Development Bank is supporting climate adaptation in agriculture in the context of the water–energy–food security nexus. The technical assistance program, which runs from April 2020 to March 2025, aims to realize the GMS vision of being a leading supplier of safe, quality, and climate-friendly agri-food products, increasing investments, and making the subregion's agri-food value chains sustainable.

Source: Asian Development Bank.

---

16 ADB. 2022. ADB Plans $14 Billion to Ease Food Crisis, Promote Long-Term Food Security in Asia and the Pacific. News release. 27 September.
17 ADB. *Agriculture and Food Security-ADB's Long Term Strategy.* Manila.

3 GOOD HEALTH AND WELL-BEING

Progress on SDG 3 in Asia and the Pacific can mainly be attributed to improved access to essential health services. However, there are still marked inequities in access and availability of affordable and high-quality health care for all communities. ADB is working with governments to achieve universal health coverage in the region and supports projects and initiatives, including through public–private partnerships, that help make health services more efficient, accessible, and equitable.[18]

During the COVID-19 pandemic, ADB committed more than $20 billion in assistance to its DMCs. In 2020, ADB launched a $9 billion Asia Pacific Vaccine Access Facility (APVAX) to secure access to affordable COVID-19 vaccines for DMCs across the region.

There are numerous examples of DMC-targeted support with a focus on SDG 3. Papua New Guinea's health sector faces a shortage of resources as the government grapples with mobilizing domestic revenue and the impacts of macroeconomic instability. In 2023, ADB approved a $42 million financing package for Papua New Guinea's Health Services Sector Development Program. The package includes a $35 million concessional loan and a $7 million grant from the ADF, which provides grants to ADB's poorest and most vulnerable DMCs. The program combines a policy-based loan and project financing to support critical sector reforms and investments in Papua New Guinea's health sector.

In India, the Strengthening Comprehensive Primary Health Care in Urban Areas Program, a results-based loan, has been supporting the government since 2021 to improve equitable access to primary health care in urban areas. The program aims to increase the number of functional health and wellness centers to cater to 256 million urban dwellers, including 51 million urban slum dwellers in 13 states in India. The project includes a comprehensive range of primary health care—preventive, promotive, and curative—for the urban population, especially poor and vulnerable people, and at no cost for patients.

Box 3: Global Climate and Health Initiative

Asia and the Pacific faces serious challenges due to climate change, which profoundly impacts public health issues by increasing the frequency and severity of disasters such as floods, storms, and heat waves. These events not only cause immediate injuries and fatalities but also have long-term impacts on mental health, food security, and the spread of infectious diseases.

Against this background, the Asian Development Bank (ADB) launched the Global Climate and Health Initiative (CHI) at the latest climate summit convened by the United Nations, COP28 in 2023, marking a significant step forward in addressing the intertwined challenges of climate change and public health. The initiative aims to consolidate policies and practices at the nexus of climate change and health through collaboration with governments, international organizations, academia, and the private sector. It will generate new knowledge, mobilize financing, build capacity, spur innovation, forge new partnerships, and champion advocacy. There is an initial $7 million in seed funding to catalyze at least $10 for each $1 through cofinancing and co-investments. ADB is also committed to dedicating at least 15% of its annual health portfolio to supporting climate-focused projects to improve the skills of health leaders to address the health consequences of climate change and to green the health sector.

Source: Asian Development Bank.

[18] ADB. 2022. *Strategy 2030 Health Sector Directional Guide: Toward the Achievement of Universal Health Care Coverage in Asia and the Pacific.* Manila.

4 QUALITY EDUCATION

Despite improving access to and participation in education, improving its quality at all levels remains a challenge. The COVID-19-induced disruption to school systems is estimated to reduce lifetime earnings in Asia and the Pacific by 5.4%.[19] ADB has been working for more than 50 years to promote quality and accessible education for all. Guided by learnings since the COVID-19 pandemic, ADB's work on education aims to transform education systems.

Bangladesh was among the countries with the longest school closures during the COVID-19 pandemic. This caused significant learning losses and, in some cases, contributed to an increase in dropouts. The COVID-19 pandemic also reduced household incomes, which is a major cause for children to discontinue enrollment in schools. The Fourth Primary Education Development Program is the government's flagship initiative aiming to provide quality education to all children. To support this program, ADB approved a concessional loan of $500 million from ADB's ordinary capital resources during 2018-2024.

Solomon Islands is a young and fast-growing country, and there is a growing need for access to quality education and better job opportunities for young people. However, this is challenging due to the archipelago's unique geography and high vulnerability to climate change. To tackle this, ADB approved $35 million to improve Solomon Islands' education sector in 2023. An estimated 18,000 secondary education students will benefit from a new national curriculum by 2030. More than 9,000 female students will complete their senior secondary education, and more than 100 female school leaders are expected to complete professional development.

To address the mismatch between university education and desired skills in the job market in the region, ADB's technical assistance program Promoting Learning and Innovation in Education to Future-Proof the Workforce was launched in 2022. It provides support to DMCs in advancing equitable learning recovery by assessing learning needs, fostering a learning-friendly environment, and developing a sustainable learning recovery pilot project.

Box 4: Indonesia's Boosting Productivity Through Human Capital Development Program

The economic slump triggered by the coronavirus disease pandemic has had a significant and possibly lasting impact on Indonesia's labor market. The situation is particularly concerning given that women's labor market participation rate had already been low. The pandemic's impacts threatened to widen gender disparities, particularly affecting women's job prospects in sectors such as accommodation and food service activities.

To address this issue, in 2021, the Asian Development Bank approved the Boosting Productivity Through Human Capital Development Program, a $500 million policy-based loan to boost Indonesia's human capital and improve labor productivity. The program uses the Sustainable Development Goals (SDGs) as an overarching framework to support labor productivity in Indonesia and facilitates integrated reforms in education, skills development, health, and social protection aligned with the SDGs. These reforms have helped strengthen policies for financing and monitoring SDG implementation, including the establishment of 48 new SDG centers in Indonesia. The centers will further localize the SDGs through research and education, outreach, and policy advice. At the same time, the government has provided performance-based fiscal transfers to local government units to incentivize progress toward achieving the SDGs at the local level.

Source: Asian Development Bank.

[19] A. Abiad et al. 2021. Inadequate Learning, Loss of Earnings: The Staggering Cost of School Closures in Asia. Asian Development Blog. 28 April.

5 GENDER EQUALITY

Despite some progress, gender inequality remains an issue, particularly when it comes to economic opportunities, and voice and influence in society. Female labor force participation rates in the region are still lower than those for men, and domestic labor and unpaid services are still mostly performed by women, aggravating existing disparities.

Global warming is exposing large populations to heat stress in countries in Asia and the Pacific with subsequent social, ecological, and economic impacts. ADB's 2023 regional technical assistance Strengthening Women's Resilience to Heat Stress will enhance the knowledge and capacity of DMCs on gender-responsive heat action planning, implementation and monitoring; and implementation of priority women-focused actions from the heat action plans. The program will be implemented in Bangladesh, Cambodia, Pakistan, Sri Lanka, and Tajikistan.

The ADF has proven instrumental in shifting portfolios to pursue more ambitious and transformative gender project designs. ADF 13, covering the period 2021–2024, was the first one to include an SDG 5 thematic pool so that grant funds can be used to support projects that pursue transformative gender approaches. Allocations under the SDG 5 window have supported a series of stand-alone transformative gender projects in Cambodia, Maldives, Nepal, Pakistan, Tajikistan, and Tonga.

Gender-based violence disproportionately affects women and girls. ADB is committed to strengthening protection against gender-based violence in its

ADB invests in women as agents of change, challenging social norms, and with ambitious corporate targets to ensure that women and girls are front and center of its investments.

Box 5: Community Resilience Partnership Program

Climate hazards are increasing and projected to become more frequent and severe with impacts leading to reduced agricultural and labor productivity, loss of livelihoods, and human displacement. Gender inequalities and climate change are threatening traditional livelihoods like fishing and farming and impacting food availability. Women often lack access to resources and decision-making power, which makes them more vulnerable to climate impacts. At the same time, women demonstrate resilience and adaptability to develop innovative strategies, such as diversifying their sources of income, using climate-smart agriculture, and preserving traditional knowledge.

Launched in 2021, the Community Resilience Partnership Program (CRPP) is designed to address these critical issues at the nexus of climate, poverty, and gender across Asia and the Pacific. Backed by the Green Climate Fund, a fund established within the framework of the United Nations Framework Convention on Climate Change, with $120 million dedicated to climate adaptation, the CRPP aims to contribute to transformational change by mobilizing large-scale public investments that support community-level adaptation of poor and vulnerable people. The program centers on developing national and local policies, plans, and programs that promote financing for community-led adaptation and increasing the meaningful participation of poor women and men in resilience-related decision-making. One of the expected outcomes is to increase the voice of women so that resilience strategies become more effective and inclusive and adequately reflect women's perspectives and needs.

Source: Asian Development Bank.

operations and has developed operational approaches and grievance redress mechanisms to mitigate and address risks of sexual exploitation, abuse, and harassment in ADB-financed projects with civil works, starting with pilot projects in Mongolia, Nepal, the Philippines, Solomon Islands, and Tajikistan.[20]

Estimates show that almost 70% of women-owned small and medium-sized enterprises (SMEs) in the formal sector in developing countries are unserved or underserved and have a financing gap of $1.7 trillion. Since 2021, Women's Finance Exchange, an ADB initiative to support financial institutions and their women borrowers, has aimed to reduce the gender gap in financial inclusion in Asia and the Pacific to ensure women have equal opportunities to access and benefit from financial services.

Over the past 5 years, ADB has put a greater focus on gender-lens investing. The bank is integrating the gender-lens investing assessment process into all new private sector transactions to identify client companies that are committed to advancing opportunities for women. In 2022, some 81% of private sector operations were gender mainstreamed.[21] ADB is part of the 2XChallenge, a partnership of development finance institutions and private sector investors committed to collectively mobilize private sector investments for women in developing country markets.

11 SUSTAINABLE CITIES AND COMMUNITIES

The region includes the world's most populated and densest cities, and some of the most fragile urban areas in the small island developing states. Rapid and often unplanned urbanization has caused a growing infrastructure deficit, increasing the risks of climate change impacts and disasters, environmental stress, and challenges with aging communities, inequitable development, and poor public transport.

ADB's Strategy 2030 identifies "Making Cities More Livable" as one of its seven operational priorities (Operational Priority 4).[22] ADB supports cities by improving their urban infrastructure and services, fostering inclusive, participatory, and integrated planning and services while becoming resilient to disasters, climate change, and to other shocks such as pandemics. It also promotes regional value chains and global production networks, along with strengthening municipal finance, governance, and citizen engagement.

The COVID-19 pandemic exposed the vulnerabilities of the region's cities, which were hit the hardest being on the front line of containment efforts. ADB's regional technical assistance Creating Investable Cities Initiative, has helped cities coordinate their planning, funding, and financing efforts to address bottlenecks that impede the private and climate financing they need to meet their 2030 nationally determined contributions (NDCs) and achieve the SDGs. Launched at the World Cities Summit 2022, the initiative helps leading cities in Georgia, India, Indonesia, Malaysia, Mongolia, and Viet Nam generate a pipeline of bankable projects aligned with the Paris Agreement on urban mobility, social housing, the circular economy, and waste management.

Housing is a key aspect of SDG 11, and ADB works in several DMCs to ensure access to quality and affordable housing. In Georgia for example, the housing sector is riddled with problems. In December 2018, ADB approved a $22.9 million loan to Credo Bank, a commercial bank, for Low-income Housing Finance to facilitate the introduction of home improvement and mortgage loan products targeting lower-income households in rural regions. The program is designed to empower women and as of 2023, the project had helped more than 13,000 women heading rural households.[23]

20 ADB. 2023. *Integrating Sexual Exploitation, Abuse, and Harassment Reporting and Case Handling into Project Grievance Redress Mechanisms: Good Practice Note for ADB-Financed Projects with Civil Works.* Manila.

21 ADB. 2023. *Private Sector Operations in 2022: Report on Development Effectiveness.* Manila.

22 ADB. 2022. *Strategy 2030 Urban Sector Directional Guide: Toward Making Cities More Livable in Asia and the Pacific.* Manila.

23 ADB. 2023. In Georgia, ADB Helped 13,000 Women Gain Access to Affordable Housing. Project Result/Case Study. 21 September.

Country Spotlight: Mongolia

SDG Progress

SDG = Sustainable Development Goal.
Source: ESCAP.

SDG implementation

Mongolia has reached some impressive milestones in its SDG implementation. It was one of the first countries in the world to adopt an SDG alignment strategy in 2016. In addition, the country endorsed the draft of Integrated National Financing Strategy (INFS) in 2022, making it also one of the early adopters of the INFS, a key vehicle for mobilizing, aligning, and leveraging resources for SDGs. Mongolia presented its first Voluntary National Review (VNR), a review of national progress toward the SDGs, in 2019 and the second such review in 2023.

Highlights of ADB's support

ADB's country partnership strategy 2021–2024 for Mongolia has three strategic priorities: fostering inclusive social development and economic opportunity; climate-resilient infrastructure to drive competitiveness and diversification; and resilience for sustainable, green, and climate-conscious development.

ADB is supporting Mongolia, in collaboration with United Nations Development Programme, under the regional TA: Advancing the 2030 Agenda for Sustainable Development, to develop a monitoring and evaluation framework for its financing strategy for the medium-term development plan, nationally determined contributions (NDCs), and SDGs, and a pilot of the SDGs taxonomy in the finance sector with commercial banks. Under another technical assistance project, Supporting Inclusive and Sustainable Development, ADB is facilitating the creation of a framework to review standards for sustainability, SDG, and green bonds.

Climate change has reduced the health and productivity of Mongolia's fragile rangelands. In 2023, the Government of Mongolia and ADB initiated the Aimags and Soums Green Regional Development Investment Program with an ADB loan of $448 million to support green and inclusive development at the subnational level.

In 2022, ADB approved an $18 million loan as part of the Tavan Bogd COVID-19 Food Security and Inclusive Job Creation Project. This followed a $15 million loan in 2020 to Ulaanbaatar Flour and Tavan Bogd Foods to sustain their operations during the COVID-19 pandemic. The project contributed to ensuring a stable supply of wheat flour, the main staple in Mongolia.

Highlighted results from completed operations (2016–2023)

- **5.4 million people benefiting from improved health services, education services, or social protection**
- **778,000 women and girls with increased resilience to climate change, disasters, and other external shocks**
- **4.4 million people benefiting from strengthened environmental sustainability**
- **668,000 people benefiting from improved services in urban areas**

Source: ADB's Development Effectiveness Review.

Regional progress

The region's emissions have seen a worrying rise of around 20% during 2010–2022, reflecting intense industrial activity, energy consumption, and significant deforestation.[24] The region is being severely affected by the consequences of climate change. In 2023 alone, over 100 disasters occurred, affecting over 47 million people and causing billions of dollars in economic losses (footnote 4).

The COVID-19 pandemic worsened the already alarming plastic pollution of rivers and oceans, due to the surge in medical-related single-use plastics.[25] Overfishing is also a major issue and has caused fish stocks to wither, placing livelihoods at risk. Preserving biodiversity is another major challenge, and the percentage of key biodiversity areas protected remains low.

Key features of ADB's approach

Strategy 2030's Operational Priority 3 aims to tackle climate change, build climate and disaster resilience, and enhance environmental sustainability, and over the years, there has been a strong focus on ensuring each climate action investment is monitored using meaningful results-based climate indicators.

Recognizing the critical importance of addressing climate change, ADB has stepped up as the climate bank for Asia and the Pacific. In 2023, ADB increased its climate ambition to deliver $100 billion of cumulative climate finance to its DMCs during 2019–2030. Separately, three out of four new operations will support climate action by 2030.[26] By 2024, ADB will have fully aligned its new nonsovereign operations with the Paris Agreement, following an alignment of new sovereign operations in 2023.

Recognizing the critical importance of addressing climate change, ADB increased its climate ambition to deliver $100 billion of cumulative climate finance to its DMCs during 2019-2030.

[24] ESCAP. 2023. SDG 13: Climate Change.

[25] EU–ASEAN Business Council. 2022. *Fighting the Plastic Pandemic.* Singapore.

[26] This target is based on a 3-year rolling average.

ADB's Impact

(accumulated results from completed operations in 2016–2023)

12 RESPONSIBLE CONSUMPTION AND PRODUCTION

- 30.1 million people benefiting from strengthened environmental sustainability

13 CLIMATE ACTION

- 18.5 million women and girls with increased resilience to climate change, disasters, and other external shocks[a]
- 28.1 million people with strengthened climate and disaster resilience
- 108.1 million tCO_2e/year total annual greenhouse gas emissions reduction

14 LIFE BELOW WATER **15 LIFE ON LAND**

- 680,000 hectares of terrestrial, coastal, and marine areas conserved, restored, and/or enhanced[a]

15 LIFE ON LAND

- 398,000 hectares of land area with reduced flood risks

tCO_2e = total carbon dioxide emissions.

[a] Figure does not include data from 2016 to 2018 as indicator was introduced in ADB's corporate results framework 2019-2024.

Source: ADB's Development Effectiveness Review.

Lost home. A family stands next to their earthquake-damaged house near Naglebhare, Nepal. The ADB-supported Earthquake Emergency Assistance Project provided urgent support to help save lives during the disaster relief period (photo by Samir Jung Thapa).

Highlights of ADB projects

12 RESPONSIBLE CONSUMPTION AND PRODUCTION

Population growth and rapid urbanization have created unsustainable patterns of consumption and production which have contributed to a massive rise in greenhouse gas (GHG) emissions. ADB is working on tackling these challenges through different sectoral initiatives. Internally, ADB continues to put a strong focus on sustainable practices to reduce its corporate carbon footprint. Every 2 years, it publishes a sustainability report in accordance with the UN Global Reporting Initiative's guidelines and centered around the SDGs.[27]

The pandemic had a devastating effect on Asia's tourism industry. In 2020, arrivals by international visitors dropped by 82% and tourism's contribution to regional GDP plummeted by 53%.[28] In December 2021, ADB set up the Southeast Asia Sustainable Tourism Facility, a $1.7 million technical assistance facility to accelerate Southeast Asia's tourism recovery from the pandemic. The facility helps countries identify and prepare environmentally sustainable tourism projects and catalyze private financing to support them.

The accumulation of waste in small island developing states (SIDS) presents massive health and environmental challenges. In 2020, ADB approved a $73 million financial package to develop a waste-to-energy facility in Maldives. The planned facility will be constructed using only a small area for waste disposal and produce renewable energy, thus addressing the country's critical land and electricity constraints. The waste-to-energy facility will be a vital component of an integrated solid waste management system, which will significantly improve public and environmental health, especially ocean health.

To support circular economy solutions and responsible consumption and production, ADB has implemented the Green Circular Economy Zero Waste Cities technical assistance program in the People's Republic of China (PRC) since 2020. The program focuses on advancing circular production, improving waste management and resource recovery, addressing e-commerce waste, and building institutional capacity. This holistic approach integrates environmental and social costs into economic activities, aiming to optimize resource use, minimize waste, and internalize external costs.

13 CLIMATE ACTION

Asia and the Pacific is home to six of the top 10 global carbon dioxide (CO_2)-emitting countries, and it accounts for more than 55% of global GHG emissions.[29] Across countries, as in the region overall, performance on climate action is unequivocally worse than on any other SDG.[30]

The battle against climate change will be won or lost in Asia and the Pacific and ADB, as the region's climate bank, has intensified its climate action ambition and support in recent years. In 2023 ADB released its Climate Change Action Plan (CCAP), 2023–2030 which outlines how it will deliver on its climate finance commitments and ambitions.

In a commitment to bold climate action, ADB's first climate action policy-based loan of $250 million, approved in 2022 and prepared jointly with Agence Française de Développement, will support the Philippines develop, deliver, and finance a holistic approach to address climate change by transitioning to low-carbon pathways, strengthening the ability of vulnerable sectors to adapt to climate change, and increasing conservation of land and marine resources.

In 2019, ADB established NDC Advance, a technical assistance platform to help DMCs mobilize finance, build capacity, and provide knowledge to implement their NDCs under the Paris Agreement. In 2022, the platform supported climate interventions in 12 DMCs, and ADB expanded its scope to help DMCs identify the investments, policy, and institutional reforms needed to slash barriers to climate adaptation investments.

---

27 ADB. *ADB Sustainability Report*. Manila (9 years: 2009–2022).

28 ADB Southeast Asia Development Solutions (SEADS). 2021. New ADB Facility to Help Southeast Asia Revive Tourism and Boost Sustainable, Inclusive Investments. 20 December.

29 ESCAP. 2022. *Protecting Our Planet through Regional Cooperation and Solidarity in Asia and the Pacific*. Bangkok.

30 ESCAP. 2023. *Asia and the Pacific SDG Progress Report: Championing SustainabilityDespite Adversities 2023*. Bangkok.

Box 6: Integrating Gender and Social Inclusion Dimensions in Climate Change Interventions

The coronavirus disease pandemic affected women, men, and vulnerable populations differently because of structural inequalities within societies in Southeast Asia. Climate change and environmental degradation are likely to exacerbate gender gaps and social inequality.

To narrow the risks of egregious inequity, the Asian Development Bank is integrating mechanisms for gender equality and social inclusion into its climate project designs. The technical assistance project Integrating Gender and Social Inclusion Dimensions in Climate Change Interventions in Southeast Asia, launched in 2022, has aimed to enhance the capacity of Southeast Asian countries to integrate gender and social inclusion in climate change policies and actions. The project aims to refine developing member countries' (DMCs) policy frameworks for integrating gender and social inclusion aspects into climate change interventions and bolster the institutional capacity of relevant government agencies and ministries. Additionally, it will foster knowledge sharing and regional cooperation toward a gender and socially inclusive green transformation. The program also supports the development of new insights into the interplay between climate action and gender and social inclusion within the Southeast Asian DMCs' context. This is achieved through conducting gender and social inclusion diagnostics in sectors crucial to achieving a net-zero transition.

Source: Asian Development Bank.

Disaster risk management is a key area of focus in ADB's climate action interventions. Southeast Asia has some of the world's most extensive transboundary disaster risk. Through the technical assistance program Strengthening Cooperation on Disaster Risk Management, launched in 2023, in partnership with the ASEAN Secretariat and the international development agency Cufa, ADB engaged 10 CSOs to help integrate social protection into disaster risk management programs in Cambodia, Indonesia, the Lao People's Democratic Republic (Lao PDR), Malaysia, the Philippines, Thailand, and Viet Nam, supporting the implementation of community-based approaches to social protection, reaching the most vulnerable people.

Home to the largest ice reserves outside of the polar regions, the Hindu Kush Himalayas feed 10 major rivers which sustain the livelihoods of more than 1.6 billion people across Asia.[31] The region is warming faster than the global average and if global temperature rises hit 3°C, 75% of glaciers in Bhutan and Nepal could melt by the end of this century.[32] ADB's 2023 technical assistance program Building Adaptation and Resilience in the Hindu Kush Himalayas is helping assess and manage climate and disaster risks in the Hindu Kush Himalayan region and will undertake in-depth analysis of multi-hazard risks and vulnerabilities in Bhutan and Nepal.

In the Kyrgyz Republic, about 550 settlements, housing 30,000 people, face immediate landslide risks.[33] Climate change is expected to increase landslide frequency because of earlier snowmelt, melting permafrost, and more intense precipitation. ADB's first integrated preemptive landslide risk reduction project approved in 2021, Managing and Preventing Landslide Risk, aims to

The battle against climate change will be won or lost in Asia and the Pacific and ADB, as the region's climate bank, has intensified its climate action ambition and support in recent years.

31 ADB. 2023. *Technical Assistance for Building Adaptation and Resilience in the Hindu Kush Himalayas—Bhutan and Nepal*. Manila.

32 ADB. 2023. ADB to Help Strengthen Climate Resilience in Hindu Kush Himalayas. News release. 3 December.

33 ADB. 2023. *Atlas of Landslides in the Kyrgyz Republic.* Manila.

safeguard rural communities in the Kyrgyz Republic. This innovative project will embed international best practices and advanced technologies for improved risk reduction and monitoring. It will combine engineering and nature-based solutions with community-based planning and capacity building for sustainable long-term landslide safety.

ADB also leads investments in other important areas of the energy transition. In Viet Nam, for example, the transport sector accounts for 18% of the country's GHG emissions, and the sector's decarbonization will directly impact the country's ambition to achieve net-zero emissions by 2050.[34] Through the VinFast Electric Mobility Green Loan Project, in 2023, ADB provided $135 million in financing to VinFast, Viet Nam's first domestic car company and e-vehicle manufacturer, to build the country's first fully electric public transport bus fleet and national e-vehicle charging network. It includes a technical assistance program focused on raising consumer awareness about e-mobility's economic, environmental, and social impacts.[35]

14 LIFE BELOW WATER

Asia and the Pacific is struggling to meet key SDG 14 targets related to marine pollution, preservation of coastal zones, and the sustainable management of marine resources.[36] Asia is estimated to account for more than 80% of all plastics released into the world's oceans.[37]

In recent years, ADB has become a leader in putting the health of the oceans at the heart of sustainability agendas. Through its $5 billion Action Plan for Healthy Oceans and Sustainable Blue Economies, launched in 2019, ADB is protecting and restoring coastal and marine ecosystems, promoting inclusive livelihood opportunities, growing sustainable blue economies, building resilient coastal communities, and contributing to food security in Asia and the Pacific.

One challenge with blue finance in Asia and the Pacific is that there is a limited pipeline of bankable ocean conservation projects that can generate returns for investors. Since 2020, following Blue Natural Capital Financing Facility's Blue Bond Guidelines, ADB has signed a number of "blue loans." The loans have focused on boosting the recycling capacities in countries such as India, Indonesia, the Philippines, and Thailand. Additionally, ADB is part of the Blue Finance Accelerator initiative, along with United Nations Development Programme (UNDP), Indonesia's Coordinating Ministry of Maritime and Investment and Instellar Indonesia, a consultancy, for startups and SMEs operating in blue sectors.

ADB has also established several blue finance facilities in recent years. The Blue Southeast Asia Finance Hub, the Blue Pacific Finance Hub, and the more recent Ocean Resilience and Coastal Adaptation Trust Fund, are all increasing the quantity and quality of investments in ocean health and coastal adaptation.

There have also been impactful projects at the country level. Cambodia's fisheries sector accounts for 8%–10% of the country's GDP.[38] However, the sector has experienced a decline in fish stocks due to overfishing and ecosystem degradation. The 2022 Sustainable Coastal and Marine Fisheries Project financed by a $41 million loan from ADB, a $22 million grant from the ADF, and a $10 million loan from the ASEAN Infrastructure Fund, aims to provide support to Cambodia's four coastal provinces to reverse the decline in fisheries, promote sustainable mariculture, and enhance fish landing sites for improved seafood safety, targeting a 30% increase in fish biomass. The project seeks to mobilize climate-resilient commercial investments.

---

34 ADB Southeast Asia Development Solutions (SEADS). 2022. ADB Leads $135 Million Climate Financing Package to Support Electric Mobility in Viet Nam. 8 November.

35 ADB. 2022. ADB Leads $135 Million Climate Financing Package to Support Electric Mobility in Viet Nam. News release. 24 October.

36 ESCAP. 2022. *SDG 14: Life Below Water.* Bangkok.

37 L. Meijer et al. 2021. More Than 1000 Rivers Account for 80% of Global Riverine Plastic Emissions into the Ocean. *Science Advances.* 7 (18).

38 Economic Research Institute for ASEAN and East Asia. 2023. Sustainable Blue Economy Development in Cambodia: Status, Challenges, and Priorities. *Policy Brief. No. 2023-06.* Jakarta.

15 LIFE ON LAND

In 2020, Asia and the Pacific recorded the world's highest number of threatened species (12,523). Between 2000 and 2015, the regional net loss in natural forests accounted for 10.6% of the world's total.[39] Freshwater ecosystems are threatened by pollution and overextraction for drinking water, energy production, and irrigation.

ADB has long been committed to protecting natural capital and biodiversity to support economic growth and improve people's lives throughout the region. This includes management of protected areas, safeguarding watersheds, restoring habitats, and conserving biodiversity.

The PRC faces rural poverty due to fragmented land plots and adverse trends in the forestry sector. The forestry sector has grown, but the current low quality of forest structure remains. From 2010 to 2019, the Forestry and Ecological Restoration Project in Three Northwest Provinces aimed to improve forestry sector productivity, demonstrate an integrated ecosystem management approach, and introduce forest carbon sequestration and climate change mitigation measures. The project contributed to carbon sequestration of 645,200 tons of CO_2, and the increase of protection of ecologically sensitive areas by 141,450 hectares. The project also enabled participating farmers and beneficiaries to better adapt to climate change by introducing sustainable land and management practices. The average net income of beneficiary households increased by 190% and rural employment increased by 99,800 jobs by 2018.

The wetlands of the East Asian-Australasian Flyway span 22 countries and support over 50 million migratory waterbirds from 210 species, 20% of which are globally threatened.[40] These wetlands provide essential ecosystem services like flood regulation and carbon sequestration. However, wetland loss and degradation continue due to agriculture and climate change, with the hunting of waterbirds remaining a major threat. In 2021, ADB launched the regional technical assistance: Scaling Up the East Asian-Australasian Flyway Initiative to preserve wetlands across Asia and the Pacific. Through an alliance with BirdLife International, a nature conservation partnership, and the East Asian–Australasian Flyway Partnership secretariat, the initiative aims to mobilize $3 billion over the next 10 years to help protect priority wetland clusters along the East Asian–Australasian Flyway.

ADB has long been committed to protecting natural capital and biodiversity to support economic growth and improve people's lives throughout the region.

39 ESCAP. 2023. SDG 15: Life on Land.
40 ADB. 2021. Regional: Scaling Up the East Asian-Australasian Flyway Initiative.

Country Spotlight: Timor-Leste

SDG Progress

SDG = Sustainable Development Goal.
Source: ESCAP.

SDG implementation

Following the adoption of the 2030 Agenda, the Government of Timor-Leste in 2015 passed a resolution establishing a working group on SDG implementation headed by the Prime Minister's Office. It also issued a decree mandating that the SDGs be reflected in annual plans and budgets. The national SDGs road map, published in 2017, sets out how the global goals align with Timor-Leste's Strategic Development Plan (SDP 2011–2030).

Timor-Leste prepared its first voluntary national review (VNR) in 2019. The review centered on the theme "From Ashes to Reconciliation, Reconstruction and Sustainable Development" and focused on laying the foundations for peace, institutions, and justice (SDG 16). The second VNR, published in 2023, revolved around steps toward people-centered sustainable development and "Leaving No One Behind," the central, transformative promise of the 2030 Agenda.

ADB's support

ADB's country partnership strategy (2023–2027) for Timor-Leste aims to support the country's economic recovery, by building climate-resilient infrastructure and basic services and promoting an enabling environment for economic diversification.

Timor-Leste's Strategic Development Plan 2011–2030 identifies access to safe water as a reform critical for the country's development. In 2022, ADB provided $127 million in loans for the Dili West Water Supply Project to improve access to safe and reliable water in the capital Dili, with the construction of climate-resilient infrastructure.

To address SDG 7, ADB's Power Distribution Modernization Project has since 2021 been engaged in strengthening the state-owned utility company's ability to manage the electricity grid, mitigating climate change challenges, and boosting women employment in the energy sector.

The technical assistance program Support for Achieving the Strategic Development Plan 2011–2030 and the Sustainable Development Goals, approved in 2018, helped the government strengthen development planning and improve the linkages between planning and budgeting.

Highlighted results from completed operations (2022)

- **9,000 women and girls benefiting from new or improved infrastructure**
- **18,000 people benefiting from improved services in urban areas**

Source: ADB's Development Effectiveness Review.

Regional progress

The COVID-19 pandemic pushed about 78 million people in Asia and the Pacific back into extreme poverty and created around 162 million newly poor people, particularly in South Asia. Even if the region is recovering, the ongoing cost-of-living crisis is stalling progress. Despite remarkable economic and social advances, critical gaps in social protection coverage persist. Around half the people living in the region are outside social protection schemes. The region is also characterized by high levels of income inequality which also worsened during the pandemic. The post-pandemic rebound in the labor market in Asia and the Pacific lags behind progress seen in other regions of the world and the region's labor market remains smaller than before the crisis.

Asia and the Pacific has a long way to go to achieve Goal 16. Nearly a quarter of businesses in the region have engaged in bribery. Children and adolescents are particularly vulnerable to violence and over one third of the women have faced sexual violence.[41] Formulation and implementation of policy to promote private sector development remains a challenge.

Key features of ADB's approach

Poverty reduction is at the core of ADB's work and is the focus of Strategy 2030's Operational Priority 1, which centers on human capital and social protection, quality jobs and opportunities for the most vulnerable people. Given the diversity across countries in the region, ADB prioritizes support for the poorest and most vulnerable people, including in fragile and conflict-affected situations (FCAS) and SIDS. ADB is the first multilateral development bank to support FCAS and SIDS under a single operational process, the FCAS and SIDS Approach (FSA), approved in April 2021.

Recognizing the links between the quality of governance and the capacity of ADB's DMCs to achieve the SDGs, Strategy 2030 Operational Priority 6 focuses on strengthening governance and institutional capacity, particularly through improved public sector management and financial stability.

Poverty reduction is at the core of ADB's work and is the focus of Strategy 2030's Operational Priority 1, which centers on human capital and social protection, quality jobs and opportunities for the most vulnerable people.

[41] ESCAP. 2023. SDG 16: Peace, Justice, and Strong Institutions.

ADB's Impact

(accumulated results from completed operations in 2016–2023)

1 NO POVERTY | **10 REDUCED INEQUALITIES**

- 158.9 million poor and vulnerable people with improved standards of living[a]
- 435.8 million people benefiting from improved health services, education services, or social protection

8 DECENT WORK AND ECONOMIC GROWTH

- 14.1 million jobs generated[a]
- 1.5 million skilled jobs for women generated[a]

9 INDUSTRY, INNOVATION AND INFRASTRUCTURE

- 6,000 low carbon infrastructure assets established or improved[a]

16 PEACE, JUSTICE AND STRONG INSTITUTIONS

- 1.1 million government officials with increased capacity to design, implement, monitor, and evaluate relevant measures[a]
- 7,700 entities with improved management functions and financial stability[a]
- 860 measures supported in implementation to improve capacity of public organizations to promote the private sector and finance sector[a]

ADB = Asian Development Bank.

[a] Figure does not include data from 2016 to 2018 as indicator was introduced in ADB's corporate results framework 2019-2024.

Source: ADB's Development Effectiveness Review.

Driven to succeed. Saidamo Abdulkhakova, a trolley bus driver in Tajikistan smiles after a hard day's work (photo by Nozim Kalandarov).

Highlights of ADB's projects

1 NO POVERTY

SDG 1 calls upon countries to implement nationally appropriate social protection systems for all, but to date only a handful of countries have comprehensive social protection systems with broad coverage.

Poverty reduction through human capital development and enhancing social protection has always been central to ADB's work.[42] ADB uses the Graduation Approach as a key strategy for addressing remaining poverty and reducing inequality in Asia and the Pacific. The approach is a holistic, time-bound, and carefully sequenced set of interventions aimed at placing households on an upward trajectory from poverty. "Graduation" is always context specific and implies reaching a situation where a household has an economically viable livelihood, is food secure, and is connected to essential services.[43]

The ADF provides grants to ADB's poorest and most vulnerable DMCs with the goal of reducing poverty. ADF resources come from contributions of ADB's member countries, mobilized under periodic replenishments, combined with net income transfers from ADB's ordinary capital resources.

Oftentimes a lack of understanding of options for financing long-term care (LTC) and how to operationalize LTC financing systems hinders DMCs from identifying appropriate LTC financing solutions. To tackle this issue, the technical assistance Strategies for Financing Social Protection to Achieve Sustainable Development Goals in DMCs started in 2017 and has supported DMCs review viable and sustainable sources of financing for social protection programs to achieve the SDGs. In the process of executing the project, DMCs highlighted the need for a deeper understanding and analysis of LTC financing. To respond to this challenge, ADB has facilitated training programs and policy dialogues.

Poverty and vulnerability persist in the Philippines despite the country's strong economic performance in recent years. The Expanded Social Assistance Project, from 2022, builds on a decade of ADB's support for social protection in the Philippines. The project helped establish the national poverty targeting system and supported the implementation and evaluation of the government's Pantawid Pamilyang Pilipino Program conditional cash transfer program. The proposed third phase will also help build a more integrated and efficient social protection system and finance the government's expansion of social transfers, including the social pension program.

ADB also works to reduce poverty in areas affected by conflict. In Afghanistan, an estimated 49.4% of the population lived below the poverty line in 2020.[44] Women and children are disproportionately affected. In 2023, ADB approved a package of new grants to support food security and health services and protect the welfare and livelihoods of vulnerable Afghan people, particularly women and girls, and ease the adverse impact of the ongoing humanitarian crisis.[45] The Expanding Essential Food Security and Health Services Project (Support for Afghan People) project has provided off-budget direct financing to three UN agencies, helping to bridge the financing gap for immediate support.

8 DECENT WORK AND ECONOMIC GROWTH

Rapid economic growth in Asia and the Pacific has benefited many workers, yet more than two in three workers are employed in the informal sector, and tens of millions have no job security, have low wages, have long working hours, and lack social protection.

Given that most jobs are created in the private sector, ADB works to support DMCs in improving the business environment. In Uzbekistan, for example, where the government continues to implement reforms

42 ADB. 2022. *Strategy 2030 Social Protection Directional Guide: Toward Inclusive and Resilient Social Protection*. Manila.
43 ADB. 2022. Graduation Approach: Unique Value Addition Resettlement Projects. *Development Asia*. 17 February.
44 ADB. Basic Statistics 2023 (accessed 18 April 2024).
45 ADB placed its regular assistance to Afghanistan on hold effective 15 August 2021.

to transition from a state-run to a market economy, SMEs have only limited access to the diverse finance necessary for different stages of their development. To help address some of these challenges, ADB in 2023 approved the Small and Medium-Sized Enterprises Development Program, a $100 million policy-based loan to support SMEs in Uzbekistan and spur economic growth.

In Fiji, a small Pacific island country with a population of some 900,000 people, investments from the private sector and state-owned enterprises (SOEs) have not responded in the same manner as public investment over the years. To tackle this issue, in 2017, ADB, through the Sustained Private Sector-Led Growth Reform Program in Fiji provided $280 million in regular loan financing. In collaboration with the Government of Fiji, the project aimed to enhance the quality of budget systems and institutions, improve the productivity and competitiveness of SOEs, and facilitate the creation of new businesses and formal job opportunities, including for women.

Trade-led, inclusive economic growth enhances a country's capacity to generate higher incomes and decent jobs. ADB supports $8 billion in trade annually through its Trade and Supply Chain Finance Program, which empowers countries to meet the SDGs by closing market gaps through guarantees, loans, and knowledge products. Additionally, the regional technical assistance Strengthening Knowledge in Regional Trade Agreements and International Investment Agreements for Greater Regional Integration and Promotion of SDGs in ADB Developing Member Countries (2022–2025) aims to increase intragovernmental knowledge, coordination, dispute prevention and management capabilities under trade agreements focused on promoting the SDGs.

10 REDUCED INEQUALITIES

Across Asia and the Pacific, notwithstanding the region's economic dynamism, inequality remains a major challenge. ADB's first operational priority to address remaining poverty focuses on reducing inequality and providing opportunities for the most vulnerable people. Risk and vulnerability to the impacts of COVID-19 are increased for populations living in poverty, as they have a lower capacity to take preventive measures, less access to health services, and fewer resources to cope with a reduction in income needed to meet basic needs. For such issues, CSOs often provide vital services to fill the gaps in formal social protection systems. In 2020, ADB initiated regional technical assistance with $2 million in funding, named Mitigating Impact of COVID-19 through Community-Led Interventions. This initiative worked with 10 CSOs across seven countries with the aim of supporting health care, social protection, and alternative livelihoods for vulnerable families and communities affected by the pandemic.

Around 70% of people with disabilities live in Asia and the Pacific.[46] They are among the poorest in the region and face significant challenges such as social exclusion, increased inequality, and extreme poverty. In 2021, ADB approved its road map for Strengthening Disability-Inclusive Development, 2021–2025, which sets out a practical route to greater disability inclusion in ADB projects, research, and organizational systems, focusing first on short- and medium-term actions.

The PRC has been facing an unprecedented wave of rapid urbanization, internal migration, and social transformation in recent decades. Migrants often report lower levels of well-being than urban and rural residents and limited access to social services, and there is a noticeably wider gender wage gap in urban areas. In 2022, ADB completed the technical assistance project Research to Support the Social Integration of Migrants to help the National Health Commission, responsible for migrant health, assess the well-being and social integration of migrants, evaluate international best practices, and develop policy recommendations including to better integrate migrant populations.

In many countries, the pandemic further deepened inequalities. The 2020 COVID-19 Solidarity Fund for Kazakhstan boosts the economic prospects of thousands of people, including those who lost their jobs due to the pandemic. Thousands of women, people with disabilities, and unemployed workers have benefited from skills training, including 7,000 women mentored through ADB-supported Women Entrepreneurship Development Centers.

46 ADB. 2022. *Strengthening Disability-Inclusive Development: 2021–2025 Road Map.* Manila.

16 PEACE, JUSTICE AND STRONG INSTITUTIONS

Asia and the Pacific has a long way to go to achieve the different dimensions of SDG 16.

ADB's efforts have increasingly been focused on promoting corruption-free delivery of public services, the implementation of anticorruption measures, and strengthening anti-money-laundering and tax integrity standards in DMCs. ADB also assists in reforming SOEs, decentralization, legal reform, and social protection.

ADB is partnering with the United Nations Office on Drugs and Crime (UNODC), regulators, and others, to reduce trade-based money laundering (TBML) by helping banks improve their reporting of suspicious transactions. UNODC's goAML application, an anti-money-laundering system adopted by more than 60 countries, helps governments collect and analyze data on suspicious financial transactions to produce actionable intelligence for justice systems. A pilot was implemented with authorities in Bangladesh, Mongolia, Nepal, Pakistan, and Sri Lanka. ADB has also designed and initiated the delivery of multiple capacity-building sessions on TBML to banks, regulators, law enforcement, and intelligence stakeholders.

Armenia's economy was hit hard by the COVID-19 pandemic and by conflict. In 2020, its GDP contracted by 7.2%, however, a robust fiscal performance allowed for significant fiscal stimulus, and in 2021 the economy rebounded by 5.7%.[47] In November 2022, ADB approved the Fiscal Sustainability and Financial Markets Development Program, a $100 million policy-based loan for Armenia under a new initiative aimed at enhancing the country's fiscal management and improving its financial markets. It is structured to encourage the development of liquid money markets and support a sustainable public debt securities issuance program.

In 2022, ADB conducted a governance assessment for the Kyrgyz Republic, evaluating public financial management systems and anticorruption efforts. Through the Strengthening Governance and Anti-Corruption in the Kyrgyz Republic program, ADB will support the government's anticorruption strategy and help strengthen the private sector and achieve inclusive growth.

The PRC has an increasingly mobile population and urban density has been rising sharply in recent decades, which poses a higher risk of transmission of infectious diseases. In line with the Healthy China 2030 plan, the country's vision of health care, ADB approved a $300 million loan with the aim of improving the quality of public health services. The 2022 Strengthening Public Health Institutions Building Project, addresses gaps in the public health system through investments in improving coordination between public health agencies, aligning technology and equipment to the rapid detection of infectious diseases, creating sufficient capacity of health facilities during outbreaks, and enhancing public health knowledge and skills.

ADB's efforts have increasingly been focused on promoting corruption-free delivery of public services, the implementation of anticorruption measures, and strengthening anti-money-laundering and tax integrity standards in DMCs.

47 IMF. 2023. *Armenia's Potential Growth: Long-Run Dynamics, Recent Developments, and Impact of Reforms.* Washington, DC.

Box 7: ADB-Supported Central Asia Regional Economic Cooperation Program

Many dimensions of the Sustainable Development Goals are transboundary in nature and regional cooperation is a powerful tool to tackle challenges that require the collaboration of multiple countries. The Asian Development Bank (ADB)-supported Central Asia Regional Economic Cooperation (CAREC) Program is an example of a partnership of 11 countries and development partners working together to boost economic growth and speed up poverty reduction. Since its inception in 2001, CAREC has mobilized $51.04 billion in investments. This has helped establish multimodal transportation networks, increased energy trade and security, facilitated free movement of people and freight, and laid the groundwork for economic corridor development.

The CAREC 2030 Strategy and its operational clusters and thematic areas are aligned with the SDGs to support regional actions that complement national efforts in attaining the goals of the subregion. CAREC helps member countries leverage private sector financing solutions by deploying public funds for de-risking and leveraging up private investments. In addition to promoting regional integration, including cross-border infrastructure connectivity, CAREC supports regional cooperation to help member countries achieve SDGs in the areas of water and agriculture, as well as human development sectors such as education and health.

Source: Asian Development Bank.

A mother's love. A family arrives from an interisland boat trip at the port in Honiara, Solomon Islands (photo by Luis Ascui).

Country Spotlight: Sri Lanka

SDG Progress

SDG = Sustainable Development Goal.
Source: ESCAP.

SDG implementation

Sri Lanka has taken proactive steps to implement the SDGs. The Sustainable Development Act of 2017 provided a legal framework and created the Sustainable Development Council as the focal public body for coordinating the implementation of the 2030 Agenda. A high-level interministerial Steering Committee on Sustainable Development was established in 2021 to oversee and step up interagency coordination for the SDGs.

The Government of Sri Lanka produced the Voluntary National Reviews assessing national progress on the SDGs in 2018 and again in 2022. Its vision is for an "Inclusive Transformation toward a Sustainably Developed Nation for All" where economic transformation is underpinned by green growth and social inclusivity.

ADB's support

ADB's support of the government's broad reforms and efforts to strengthen institutions has been critical for maintaining progress toward the SDGs. The key strategic objectives of the new Sri Lanka country partnership strategy for 2024–2028 are strengthening public financial management and governance, fostering private sector development promoting green growth, improving access to climate-smart public services, and deepening inclusion.

In 2022, Sri Lanka faced an unprecedented economic crisis, which severely impacted poor and vulnerable groups. In response, ADB, in 2023, extended the Economic Stabilization Program with a $350 million special policy-based loan as part of an IMF-led financial package to restore macroeconomic and financial stability and undertake structural transformation.

To address a food insecurity crisis in the country, ADB's Food Security and Livelihood Recovery Emergency Assistance Project aims to ensure access to food and protect the livelihoods of poor and vulnerable people, particularly women and children, enhancing social protection systems, and strengthening responsiveness to future emergencies.

Sri Lanka is taking steps toward an energy transition involving reducing the reliance on oil-fired power plants. Among other projects, ADB's Wind Power Generation Project, launched in 2017, aims to increase access to clean and reliable power supply.

Highlighted results from ADB's completed operations (2016–2023)

- **1.5 million people benefiting from improved health services, education services, or social protection**
- **658,000 total greenhouse gas emissions reduction (tCO_2e)**
- **1.3 million people benefiting from increased rural investment**
- **846,000 people enrolled in improved education and/or training**

Source: ADB's Development Effectiveness Review.

SUSTAINABLE INFRASTRUCTURE

6 CLEAN WATER AND SANITATION | 7 AFFORDABLE AND CLEAN ENERGY | 9 INDUSTRY, INNOVATION AND INFRASTRUCTURE

Regional progress

Well-prepared infrastructure projects can act as a powerful catalyst for achieving the SDGs. However, critical issues remain with basic infrastructure in Asia and the Pacific. Nearly 500 million people lack access to water supply systems, and 1.14 billion people live without basic sanitation facilities.[48] Furthermore, over 350 million people have limited access to electricity, and an additional 150 million have no access at all.[49] Crucially, around 85% of the energy consumed in Asia and the Pacific comes from fossil fuels.[50] As economic development and urbanization progress, the region's demand for energy is expected to almost double by 2030. Therefore, there is an urgent need to significantly increase clean and renewable energy to mitigate the impacts on the climate and the environment.

Key features of ADB's approach

Strategy 2030 affirms that ADB will promote quality infrastructure that is green, resilient, inclusive, and sustainable, to deliver its seven operational priorities and its global commitments to address climate change and the SDGs.

ADB was one of the first MDBs to develop a framework for measuring and reporting on the quality of its infrastructure investments—the green, resilient, inclusive, and sustainable (GRIS) quality infrastructure indicator. Each of the four GRIS criteria is aligned with specific SDG targets and the G20 Principles for Quality Infrastructure Investment. Since it was first introduced in 2019, the GRIS indicator has classified all ADB's infrastructure projects as "quality infrastructure."

ADB's Impact

(accumulated results from completed operations in 2016–2023)

6 CLEAN WATER AND SANITATION

- 81.1 million people benefiting from improved water supply and sanitation services
- 30.8 million people benefiting from improved flood management
- 40.3 million people benefiting from improved irrigation

7 AFFORDABLE AND CLEAN ENERGY

- 102,000 megawatts installed renewable energy capacity

9 INDUSTRY, INNOVATION AND INFRASTRUCTURE

- 6,000 low carbon infrastructure assets established or improved[a]
- 760 new and existing infrastructure assets made climate and disaster resilient[a]

ADB = Asian Development Bank.

[a] Figure does not include data from 2016 to 2018 as indicator was introduced in ADB's corporate results framework 2019-2024.

Source: ADB's Development Effectiveness Review.

48 ADB. 2022. Meeting the Challenge of Water Security and Resilience in Asia and the Pacific. Article. 20 July.

49 ADB. ADB's Work in the Energy Sector.

50 International Renewable Energy Agency (IRENA). *Asia and Pacific Overview.*

Highlights of ADB's support

6 CLEAN WATER AND SANITATION

Asia and the Pacific accounts for 36% of global freshwater resources; however, its per capita water availability is the lowest among the world's regions.[51] ADB is working to improve water security and resilience in Asia and the Pacific by supporting inclusive, resilient, sustainable, and well-governed service delivery and resource management.[52] Since 2022, ADB is a member of the Water and Climate Coalition to join forces globally and get on track in meeting the water-related SDGs, ensure resilient water adaptation to climate change, and provide efficient and sustainable water solutions to DMCs.

During the UN COP27 climate conference in 2022, ADB launched the Asia and the Pacific Water Resilience Hub, an open platform to bolster water security in the region. The hub supports access to knowledge products, innovative tools, data, and digital technologies. The initiative aims to mobilize more than $200 million during 2021–2025 to support inclusive and well-governed water services delivery and resource management to strengthen the region's water and sanitation resilience and security.

Since 2019, the focus of the cofinancing agreement with the Bill & Melinda Gates Foundation, one of the world's largest charities, under the Sanitation Financing Partnership Trust Fund, has broadened to include projects on citywide inclusive sanitation, whether sewered or non-sewered, centralized or decentralized, and providing the necessary support to increase knowledge and capacity and improve governance.

There are numerous examples of ADB projects supporting water and sanitation systems in DMCs. Nepal has experienced rapid urbanization in the past few years, but the quality and quantity of water services was inadequate. The situation was especially concerning in small towns. To tackle this, in 2022, ADB approved the Third Small Towns Water Supply and Sanitation Sector Project, a $60 million loan package in Nepal to deliver inclusive, gender-focused, and sustainable water supply and sanitation service in selected towns. The project successfully provided 71,724 household connections, including over 26,000 in poor and vulnerable households and households headed by women. The project also financed the construction of 22 water treatment plants and over 5,000 private toilets benefiting 28,987 people.

7 AFFORDABLE AND CLEAN ENERGY

As Asia and the Pacific is leading the world in rising energy demand, some of its countries have the largest gaps in energy access. The actions taken by the region's countries will greatly impact progress toward achieving SDG 7.

ADB works to improve access to reliable, affordable, low-carbon energy across the region. Through various financing instruments, the bank develops projects in renewable energy generation, energy efficiency, electricity transmission and distribution, and energy utilities. Policy and governance reform in the power sector has also been central to ADB's approach to enable markets, encourage private sector participation, and promote clean energy.[53]

ADB has launched several innovative finance strategies to support the energy transition in Asia and the Pacific (Chapter IV). A highlight is ADB's Energy Transition Mechanism, which, recognizing the importance of early retirement of coal assets to reach climate goals, has placed ADB at the forefront of climate action for the energy transition.

ADB's 2021 Energy Policy underscores ongoing commitment to SDG 7 in the critical and urgent task of transitioning to reliable, affordable, and clean energy. ADB will not support coal mining, processing, storage, and transportation, nor any new coal-fired power generation. The bank will also not support any natural gas exploration or drilling.

In 2021, ADB, together with other MDBs, committed to five high-level principles outlining the guiding framework for MDBs support to client countries to enable a just transition that promotes economic diversification and inclusion.[54] In 2022, ADB launched the Just Transition Support Platform which focuses on building the capacity

---

51 ESCAP. 2023. Water on the Global Centre Stage: Every Drop Counts. 20 March.
52 ADB. 2022. *Strategy 2030 Water Sector Directional Guide: A Water-Secure and Resilient Asia and the Pacific*. Manila.
53 ADB. Energy in Asia and the Pacific.
54 ADB. 2021. ADB Joins MDBs to Support Just Transition Toward Net-Zero Economies. News Release. 29 October.

of DMCs to strategically plan, implement, and finance a just transition to low-carbon and climate-resilient economies and societies.

There are numerous examples of renewable energy projects financed by ADB. In 2020, the South Thailand Wind Power and Battery Energy Storage Project, was the first wind power plant in Thailand to adopt energy storage system technology as the solution to the intermittency of wind power. The project is enhancing grid stability and is aligned with Thailand's clean energy ambitions. In 2021, the project won "Wind Power Project of the Year – Thailand" from the Asian Power Awards, a recognition program.

Global warming and rising sea levels make Kiribati one of the world's most climate-vulnerable countries. In 2022, ADB invested in the South Tawara Renewable Energy project, cofinanced by the Strategic Climate Fund and the Government of New Zealand, to install climate-resilient solar photovoltaic and battery storage systems, as well as provide institutional capacity building for the agencies that implement the project. The project aims to help the capital city of South Tarawa increase its renewable energy grid penetration from 9% to more than 44% (exceeding the government's target of 36% by 2025).

Cross-border electricity trade offers an important way for countries in the region to meet their growing electricity demand. ADB's 2023 Monsoon Wind Power Project is a $693 million project financing package to build a 600-megawatt wind power plant in southern Lao PDR with the aim of exporting power to neighboring Viet Nam. The project will be the country's first wind power plant and the largest in Southeast Asia. The financing from ADB and its partners will help unlock the Lao PDR's untapped wind resources and provide a basis for the country's transition to clean energy.[55]

9 INDUSTRY, INNOVATION AND INFRASTRUCTURE

Developing Asia will need to invest $13.8 trillion, or $1.7 trillion annually from 2023 to 2030, to sustain economic growth, reduce poverty, and respond to climate change.[56] ADB plays an important role in supporting sustainable infrastructure finance and development as a source of growth for the region.[57]

Many countries in Asia and the Pacific are exploring innovative financing mechanisms and partnerships with development agencies and the private sector to mobilize capital to bridge the infrastructure investment gap and support their economic development. ADB's Leading Asia's Private Infrastructure Fund, established in 2016, and relaunched in 2023, with support from the Japan International Cooperation Agency, leverages and complements ADB's existing nonsovereign platform to fill financing gaps and increase access to finance for infrastructure projects in the region. In 2021, ADB launched a partnership with Temasek, HSBC, and Clifford Capital to continue finding solutions to unlock Asia's critical sustainable infrastructure requirements.

In 2022, ADB approved the South Commuter Railway Project, a $4.3 billion facility to support the Philippines in financing the construction of a 54.6-kilometer railway, connecting Metro Manila and Calamba, located in Laguna Province, and includes 18 stations easily accessible for older people, women, children, and people with disabilities. The project will provide affordable, reliable, and safe public transport; reduce GHG emissions; and cut travel times. It will create 35,500 jobs during the construction phase and 3,200 permanent jobs during operation and improve access for around 300,000 residents who work along the railway line.

Nepal was hit by the most devastating earthquake in its history in 2015. Hundreds of thousands of people were left homeless. The education of about 1.5 million children was affected.[58] In response, ADB launched the Earthquake Emergency Assistance Project and provided a quick-disbursing grant to help save lives during the disaster relief period. Within 9 weeks, the bank provided a $200 million emergency loan and $3.4 million in technical assistance to begin urgent reconstruction work and accelerate Nepal's recovery. The ADB project rebuilt 154 schools to disaster-resilient standards. The project also rehabilitated 301 kilometers of district roads. Some 57 severely damaged buildings, and 61 slightly damaged ones, were repaired.

---

55 ADB. 2023. ADB Signs Loan for First Cross-Border Wind Power Project in Asia, First Plant in Lao PDR and Largest in Southeast Asia. News release. 1 March.

56 ADB. 2023. *Reinvigorating Financing Approaches For Sustainable And Resilient Infrastructure in ASEAN+3.* Manila.

57 ADB. 2023. *Strategy 2030 Transport Sector Directional Guide*. Manila.

58 ADB. 2020. Five Years After the Nepal Earthquake-Building Back Better Schools for a Safer Future. Project Result/Case Study. 24 April.

Box 8: SOURCE Platform

Developing quality, reliable, sustainable, and resilient infrastructure is the first target in Sustainable Development Goal (SDG) 9 and at the same time, a means to achieve many other SDGs. For most developing countries, the main barrier to mobilizing and channeling private capital in infrastructure for the SDGs is a lack of a pipeline of well-prepared, bankable, and investable projects.

The Asian Development Bank helped create and establish SOURCE, a joint initiative of multilateral development banks, to support partner countries in designing and managing quality sustainable infrastructure projects aligned with the SDGs and other international agreements. Some 50 countries have expressed interest in using SOURCE. At the time of writing this report, six countries had fully implemented it, and 12 are in the implementation phase. The platform currently contains 2,432 projects and 4,812 users. From project definition to operation and maintenance, SOURCE allows public agencies to define clear SDG targets so that they can be integrated early at the development stage and monitored across the project life cycle. A red flag is raised when an SDG is targeted but not translated into quantified targets as part of the expected positive impacts identified at the project appraisal stage. An SDG impact dashboard for monitoring and reporting of SDG impacts is available at the portfolio level. The graphic below shows the targeted positive impacts related to SDGs already defined at stage 2 of the project pipeline.

SDG Impact Dashboard in SOURCE

Source: ADB. 2023. *SOURCE-The Multilateral Platform for Sustainable Infrastructure.* Manila. Sustainable Infrastructure Foundation

Source: Asian Development Bank.

Country Spotlight: Tajikistan

SDG Progress

SDG = Sustainable Development Goal.
Source: ESCAP.

SDG implementation

The Tajikistan National Development Strategy (NDS) 2030 was launched in 2016. Since then, several Sustainable Development Goal (SDG) targets and indicators have been incorporated into national strategies, but gaps remain. In 2017, the government formulated a National Roadmap for Financing the NDS and the SDGs to better understand the gaps and necessary steps to increase financing for development.

Tajikistan's first voluntary national review (VNR) in 2017 reported on the country's efforts to eradicate poverty and mainstreamed the SDGs in tandem with two strategic development goals identified in the NDS 2030: energy security and efficient use of electricity, and food security and quality nutrition. The second VNR, published in 2023, focuses on achievements and opportunities as the country invests more in an environmentally friendly and sustainable future.

ADB's support

ADB's country partnership strategy (2021–2025) for Tajikistan seeks to boost quality of economic growth by prioritizing three areas: supporting structural reforms to enhance the efficiency of resource allocation and mobilization amid a transition to a market economy, improving labor productivity through human capital development, and fostering better livelihoods through investment in a landlocked economy.

Tajikistan has the lowest share of people in Central Asia with access to safe water (around 55% of the population). To tackle this challenge, ADB approved a grant of $41.8 million in 2018 and additional financing of $38 million in 2022 for the Dushanbe Water Supply and Sanitation Project. The project supports the building of climate-resilient water supply and sanitation infrastructure in the capital Dushanbe.

More than 60% of economically active Tajiks work in the agriculture sector.[a] In 2022, ADB approved the Building Resilience with Active Countercyclical Expendi tures (BRACE) program to help the government expand social assistance for poor and vulnerable people, support domestic food production, safeguard small businesses, and support the jobs of returning migrants.

Despite having achieved universal access to electricity, Tajikistan's energy infrastructure is ineffective. To support the power sector, ADB approved a $105 million grant in 2020. The Power Sector Development Program aims to drive the restructuring of the existing power utilities, create a new power sector regulator, adopt a tariff methodology, and set up a centralized cash control system.

Highlighted results from completed operations (2019–2023)

- **2.7 million people benefiting from improved health services, education services, or social protection**
- **999,000 women and girls with increased resilience to climate change, disasters, and other external shocks**

[a] ADB. 2023. Tajikistan Farmers Get Affordable Financing to Boost Food Supply. Project Result/Case Study. 20 December.

Source: ADB's Development Effectiveness Review.

IV. Mobilizing Finance and Driving Knowledge for the SDGs

17 PARTNERSHIPS FOR THE GOALS

SDG 17 is a crosscutting goal with 19 targets in the areas of mobilizing finance, providing knowledge and capacity-building, promoting technology, and addressing systemic issues.

Mobilizing finance and knowledge is central to ADB's Strategy 2030, which positions the bank as an effective catalyst of finance for development, provider of knowledge, convenor of partnerships, and driver of innovative integrated solutions.[59]

ADB operates at the regional and country levels to address gaps in knowledge and data production, accessibility, and use, and supports a number of knowledge data initiatives and platforms that work to facilitate decision-makers' access to reliable and easy-to-use SDG data.

Mobilizing Finance for the SDGs

Achieving the SDGs requires an immense collaborative effort. Public finance alone cannot meet the financing needs of the SDGs, and mobilizing finance from diverse sources, particularly the private sector, is vital to achieving the 2030 Agenda.

Capital mobilization and cofinancing activities are at the core of ADB's mission. ADB employs a wide range of mechanisms to mobilize and channel finance for the SDGs at scale. Figure 12 lays out the different mechanisms ADB uses to mobilize the large amounts of finance that the SDGs require.

Figure 12: ADB's Mechanisms to Mobilize the Additional Finance that the SDGs Require

ADB = Asian Development Bank, SDG = Sustainable Development Goal.

Source: Asian Development Bank.

[59] ADB. 2022. *Strategy 2030 Finance Sector Directional Guide: Innovative and Sustainable Finance for Asia and the Pacific.* Manila.

Cofinancing partnerships

Cofinancing, a key pillar of ADB's Strategy 2030, mobilizes additional financial and technical resources for supporting DMCs. ADB targets a substantial increase in long-term cofinancing by 2030 with every $1 in financing for its private sector operations matched by $2.50 in long-term cofinancing. Through cofinancing partnerships, ADB mobilized $107.8 billion from 2016 to 2023 (as reference, ADB's total financing assistance from 2016 to 2023 amounted to $183.5 billion).

ADB partners with international development agencies and multilateral and bilateral institutions to cofinance projects. ADB also assists DMCs in gaining access to cofinancing from global funds.

ADB has actively sought to establish partnerships with the private sector and philanthropies, such as the Bill & Melinda Gates Foundation, the Global Energy Alliance for People and Planet, the Rockefeller Foundation, Bloomberg Philanthropies, and other emerging development partners.

Some examples of cofinancing partnerships have been highlighted in the previous section on ADB's contributions to different SDGs.

Expanding private sector operations

ADB's private sector operations facilitate debt and equity capital mobilization for private and state-owned companies, banks, and projects in infrastructure, financial services, clean energy, agribusiness, and other core sectors. ADB also mobilizes cofinancing via syndication and credit enhancement products.

ADB taps donor funds to expand its private sector work into newer sectors and help the private sector overcome development risks by offering financing on concessional terms and conditions to projects that would not proceed solely on a commercial basis. In these cases, ADB commits to be judicious in its use of concessional financing to not distort local markets and is guided by a set of principles on the use of concessional finance.[60]

In 2021, ADB partnered with Goldman Sachs and Bloomberg Philanthropies to launch the Climate Innovation Development Fund (CIDF). The fund has allocated $25 million in philanthropic concessional capital to help advance sustainable low-carbon economic development in South Asia and Southeast Asia. Thus far, CIDF has unlocked around $500 million in private sector and government investments.[61]

In 2022, ADB and ILX Management, a fund manager, signed cooperation arrangements to help scale up private sector investments to address climate change and other development challenges in DMCs to achieve the SDGs. The two parties collaborate in identifying projects under ADB's private sector operations that qualify for cofinancing, using ILX Fund as a vehicle for mobilization.[62]

Established in early 2020, ADB Ventures invests in early-stage companies with technology-enabled solutions that have the potential to scale and deliver climate and development impact in emerging Asia. The venture platform unlocks the potential for private sector capital and technological know-how to attain the SDGs. As of 2023, ADB Ventures has 40 successful investments in early-stage tech-based companies with a special focus on climate and gender. In 2023, the Republic of Korea pledged $3 million in cofinancing to expand the ADB Ventures Seed program.

ADB Frontier provides catalytic funding and technical support to growing SMEs that are building and transforming new local industries in small frontier markets but lack access to risk capital. ADB Frontier adopts a customized approach that allows for financial innovation and financing transactions that are highly developmental and support market development. This new initiative is initially focusing on Cambodia, Fiji, the Lao PDR, and other Pacific DMCs.

Innovative cofinancing platforms

In recent years, ADB has supported the establishment of some new cofinancing platforms in the region to scale up finance for the SDGs through innovation and partnerships.

60 ADB. 2022. *DFI Working Group on Blended Concessional Finance for Private Sector Projects: Joint Report 2021.* Manila.
61 ADB, Bloomberg Philanthropies, and Goldman Sachs. 2023. *Progress and Lessons from the Climate Innovation and Development Fund.*
62 ADB. 2022. ADB, ILX Partner to Boost Climate and Other SDG Investments in Asia and Pacific. News release. 21 April.

The Innovative Finance Facility for Climate in Asia and the Pacific (IF-CAP) is a new mechanism aimed at catalyzing climate finance for developing countries, drawing in contingent finance, guarantees, and grant resources from traditional and new partners, such as philanthropies. For every $1 that is guaranteed, $5 of new climate loans could be generated under IF-CAP's mechanism. In total, the facility aims to mobilize as much as $15 billion in financing to fund climate-focused projects in countries in Asia and the Pacific.

There are other examples of innovative finance platforms supported by ADB for the energy transition. The Energy Transition Mechanism (ETM), launched in 2021 and developed in partnership with DMCs, will leverage a market-based approach to accelerate the transition from fossil fuels to clean energy. The Energy Transition Acceleration Finance Partnership launched in December 2023, with the Global Energy Alliance for People and Planet, and the Monetary Authority of Singapore, will mobilize concessional capital from philanthropic and public sectors, de-risk projects, and crowd-in private capital from around the globe. In 2023, ADB executed a contribution agreement with the Swedish Energy Agency for the commitment of around $27 million. ADB's Climate Action Catalyst Fund, a first-of-its-kind multiple-partner carbon fund that will scale up investments to meet the objectives of the Paris Agreement and the SDGs commenced on 1 January 2024.[63] The fund aims to mobilize innovative carbon finance through the purchase of carbon credits.

Additionally, during the latest climate summit convened by the UN in 2023, COP28, ADB launched the Nature Solutions Finance Hub for Asia and the Pacific. The hub seeks to attract at least $2 billion into investments that incorporate nature-based solutions, which refers to the sustainable management and use of natural features and processes to tackle socioenvironmental issues. It aims to provide integrated activities and innovative finance structuring for nature-based solutions projects.

Box 9: SDG Indonesia One

The lack of large-scale pipeline of bankable green infrastructure projects and the underutilization of capital markets and innovative mechanisms for accessing private financing sources were identified as a key challenge in Indonesia's journey to achieve the Sustainable Development Goals (SDGs).

SDG Indonesia One is an integrated funding platform to support infrastructure development that is in line with achieving the SDGs. Supported by Asian Development Bank (ADB), ASEAN Catalytic Green Finance Facility is considered the first green finance facility in Southeast Asia.[a] Its focus areas are commercial financing, concessional funds for de-risking, equity funds, and project development with the objective to use public funding to draw in private financing to support infrastructure projects to achieve SDGs. The platform is part of a larger effort that involves leveraging ADB and government funds to attract and multiply green funds from private, institutional, and commercial sources. It aims to support Indonesia in developing a financing mechanism that can link incentivizing debt funds to projects with clear green targets, financial bankability thresholds, and road maps for private capital flows. Each project must meet clear green or SDG eligibility criteria. The platform is estimated to reduce carbon dioxide emissions by up to 480,700 tons per year.[b]

ASEAN = Association of Southeast Asian Nations.

[a] ADB. 2024. *ASEAN Catalytic Green Finance Facility: Expanding Support to Build Green Pipelines.* Manila.
[b] ADB. 2022. *SDG Indonesia One: Green Finance Facility.* Manila.

Source: Asian Development Bank.

63 ADB. 2023. ADB Announces Start of Climate Action Catalyst Fund. News release. 8 November.

Raising capital through thematic bonds

Thematic bonds continue to be instrumental in raising and directing capital toward projects that promote the SDGs. ADB issues its own theme bonds for sustainable development and supports DMCs to develop the bond market and raise capital through their own bond issuances.

As of 29 January 2024, the amount of outstanding green, blue, and other theme bonds issued by ADB was around $23 billion equivalent.[64]

In 2010, ADB launched its first theme (water) bond for sustainable development, in response to a growing investor demand. From water bonds, ADB has expanded its theme bond offerings to include health, gender, and education bonds. ADB launched its Green Bond Program in 2015 and has raised around $10 billion. The program helps finance climate change mitigation and adaptation projects (footnote 62). The Blue bond program has raised about $300 million since 2021.

Through technical assistance programs, ADB has created greater supply and demand for local currency-denominated sustainable bonds and scaled up GSS+ bonds issuances across Southeast Asia. ADB has also supported the ASEAN Capital Market Forum which has produced tools and standards including the ASEAN SDG Bonds Toolkit.[65]

Through policy-based lending programs ADB has been supporting capital market development for thematic bonds in countries such as Bangladesh, Indonesia, Nepal, and Uzbekistan.

The SDG Accelerator Bond was proposed by ADB in 2021 as a financial instrument to help DMCs attract global private financing and accelerate progress toward the SDGs. This innovative type of SDG bond is designed to reduce the investment risk associated with entities, sectors, or projects that lack a history of bond issuance by providing credit enhancement through a guarantee fund structure.[66]

At the country level, in 2023, ADB supported the Philippines' first gender bond by a nonstock microfinance nonprofit organization and invested in the first certified gender bond in the South Caucasus. In February 2022, ADB committed the Bank of Qingdao's Blue Finance Project in the PRC.

Domestic resource mobilization

Fiscal policies are a powerful tool to help governments raise and spend their own funds to finance the SDGs and can simultaneously mobilize resources, reduce inequalities, and promote sustainable consumption and production. In 2021, ADB launched the Asia Pacific Tax Hub to provide an open and inclusive platform for strategic policy dialogue, knowledge sharing, and development coordination among ADB, its members, and development partners, on domestic resource mobilization. The hub provides support for DMCs in three priority areas: preparation of medium-term revenue strategies, support digital transformation of tax administration, and proactive participation in international tax cooperation initiatives.

At the country level, ADB has implemented several projects focused on domestic resource mobilization. A recent project in the Philippines focuses on facilitating ongoing complex and challenging domestic resource mobilization reforms through policy-based loans. The program emphasizes the importance of coordinating these efforts with stakeholders, including those focusing on gender issues and CSOs. In Solomon Islands, a $5 million program is designed to assist the government in collecting domestic revenues more efficiently. The support is aimed at funding the objectives set out in the country's long-term National Development Strategy (2016–2035), which include addressing basic needs and ensuring food security for poor and vulnerable groups.

Building a pipeline of SDG projects in DMCs

Besides the lack of available finance, one of the main barriers to driving investments toward the SDGs has been the lack of well-prepared and investment-ready projects. ADB recognizes the importance of channeling SDG finance to the right projects, both through private and public investments.

64 ADB. 2023. *ADB Theme Bonds for Sustainable Development.* Manila.
65 ASEAN Capital Markets Forum
66 ADB. 2021. *Accelerating Sustainable Development After COVID-19. The Role of SDG Bonds.* Manila.

ADB actively assists developing economies in attracting greater private investment and fostering dynamic private sector-led growth across Asia and the Pacific by supporting governments in establishing the right policy and regulatory frameworks for capital mobilization at scale.

The $78 million Asia–Pacific Project Preparation Facility is a multidonor trust fund that aims to support governments of DMCs in effectively structuring infrastructure projects that involve private sector participation. These projects encompass various models such as privatization and public–private partnerships to make the reshaped entities globally competitive. Fund support is disbursed based on a series of sustainable goals and priorities, such as projects' climate resilience, sustainability and impact on poverty reduction, enhancement of regional connectivity and regional economic integration.[67]

The digital platform SOURCE (Box 8), also helps countries build a project pipeline that is in line with private investors' needs and considers the government's SDG gaps.

The technical assistance program Accelerating Climate Transitions through Green Finance in Southeast Asia, under the ASEAN Catalytic Green Finance Facility, will provide a regional platform to help DMCs in Southeast Asia mobilize public and private finance for commitments under the Paris Agreement and the SDGs. The program aims to strengthen upstream planning, project origination, and capacity to accelerate a pipeline of green projects for the region. It will provide integrated support across several stages of the project cycle: country planning and programming, origination, preparation, and implementation.

To fill the SME and natural capital financing gap in Asia and the Pacific, ADB, jointly with United Nations Environment Programme and UNDP, developed SME Blue Impact Asia. The digital blended finance platform is building a pipeline of investable opportunities and uses the SDGs as a framework. The scope of the projects ranges from seaweed farming and seafood processing to blockchain technology for the seaweed industry.

[67] ADB. 2022. *Asia–Pacific Project Preparation Facility.* Manila.

Beautifully blue. Fish of different kinds provide beautiful colors to the marine life in Batangas, Philippines (photo by Brian Manuel).

Country Spotlight: Pacific DMCs

SDG Progress

SDG = Sustainable Development Goal.
Source: ESCAP.

SDG implementation

The Pacific Islands Forum Leaders committed to the implementation of the Sustainable Development Goals (SDGs) in 2015, while calling for the goals to be adapted to the unique conditions of the countries in the Pacific. The Pacific Islands Forum Secretariat is the key institution facilitating regional coordination and exchange of good practices between countries to achieve the 2030 Agenda. The Pacific Sustainable Development Report 2018 (PSDR) is the first quadrennial progress report. The 2020 biennial PSDR outlines the most recent high-level trends on progress toward the SDGs.

The 13 Pacific voluntary national reviews (VNRs) since 2016 show that while systems, policies, and processes are largely in place in most countries, there is a need to build capacity to enhance national planning, budgeting, implementation, monitoring, and reporting systems.

ADB's support

The Pacific Approach 2021–2025 serves as ADB's partnership strategy for the 12 Pacific developing member countries (DMCs) (the Cook Islands, the Federated States of Micronesia, Kiribati, the Marshall Islands, Nauru, Niue, Palau, Samoa, Solomon Islands, Tonga, Tuvalu, and Vanuatu). It focuses on three priorities: preparing for and responding to shocks, delivering sustainable services, and supporting inclusive growth. Fiji and Papua New Guinea have their own country partnership strategy.

The Pacific Disaster Resilience Program, committed in 2017, provided $54 million in grant financing to help Pacific DMCs overcome multiple crises. The grants included $10 million to support Tonga's early relief and recovery from the devastating volcanic eruption and tsunami in 2023.

In 2022, ADB committed $994.4 million to its Pacific DMCs, including $452.5 million to help them recover from the impacts of the coronavirus disease pandemic. A series of policy-based loans aim to enhance public financial management, expand private sector investment, and strengthen financial inclusion, as well as reinvigorate tourism, boost agriculture, and enhance business and trade. ADB has also continued fostering climate resilience in the Pacific, supporting environmental policy reform, the expansion of clean energy, and nature-based coastal protection.

With regard to examples of projects at country level, ADB committed $208.6 million in loans to Papua New Guinea to expand and enhance power services. The Power Sector Development project approved in 2022 aims to provide access to 56,000 new beneficiaries.

Highlights from ADB's completed operations (2016–2023)

- **970,000 people benefiting from improved health services, education services, or social protection**
- **519,000 people benefiting from improved services in urban areas**
- **$12 million additional climate finance mobilized**

Source: ADB's Development Effectiveness Review.

Driving Knowledge for SDG Achievement

Knowledge plays a pivotal role in addressing the complex challenges set forth by the SDGs. Each SDG relies on decision-making, innovation, and collaboration that only effective knowledge management can achieve. ADB's Knowledge Management Action Plan, published in 2021, recognizes the importance of knowledge to help identify where the bank can add most value in supporting DMCs achieve the SDGs.

ADB's knowledge support on SDG implementation is articulated through several technical assistance programs, led by different departments within the bank, and in coordination with a diverse group of partners. Since the SDGs were adopted, ADB has approved over 16 technical assistance programs, published over 87 knowledge products and hosted 31 events that centred around the implementation and achievement of the SDGs.

Regional SDG knowledge sharing platforms

ADB supports a range of knowledge platforms that focus on different aspects of the SDGs. The SDG Dialogues webinar series, launched in 2021, to engage senior ADB Management and global experts to reflect on challenges and opportunities for SDG attainment in the region. Four dialogues were produced in 2021 covering topics such as private sector investing on the SDGs, impact management and measurement for the SDGs, and SDG localization.

Advisory support on SDG implementation at the national level

SDG implementation refers to establishing an architecture to support the delivery of the SDGs in developing countries, integrating the SDGs into national plans, leveraging financing sources for the SDGs, developing projects and programs that will support SDG progress, and strengthening data management and reporting on SDG progress at all levels.

As part of the regional technical assistance program Advancing the 2030 Agenda for Sustainable Development, 2021–2024, ADB is working with a number of countries on SDG implementation support. In Mongolia, in collaboration with UNDP, ADB is supporting the government on its SDG financing strategy (see Country Spotlight: Mongolia). Together with Pakistan's SDG Unit in the Ministry of Planning, Development and Special Initiatives, ADB is supporting capacity development to integrate the SDGs framework into the Planning Commission Form-Tra1 (PC-1). The PC-1 is the primary planning tool for all government agencies and departments, when formulating proposals and reviewing development projects.

In 2019, ADB partnered with UNDP to develop a set of SDG implementation snapshots in Armenia, Cambodia, Indonesia, Nepal, and Pakistan, which describe the efforts each country has taken to implement the SDGs in their architecture, plans, programs and budgets, financing, and data. The snapshots were aimed to help identify where ADB could best support DMCs in implementing the 2030 Agenda, and improve links between the SDGs and ongoing and planned programming.

Box 10: Asia-Pacific SDG Partnership

The Asia-Pacific SDG Partnership is a long-standing knowledge collaboration between the Economic and Social Commission for Asia and the Pacific (ESCAP), the Asian Development Bank, and the United Nations Development Programme based on the common interest to eradicate poverty and achieve inclusive growth and Sustainable Development Goals (SDGs) in Asia and the Pacific. Since 2015, the partnership has published an annual thematic report that explores different areas of implementation of the 2030 Agenda. In 2023, the report titled, Delivering on SDGs through Solutions at the Energy, Food and Finance Nexus, analyzed the confluence of transitions needed in this nexus, and highlighted the needed solutions to advance the SDGs in the region. The most recent 2024 report, People and Planet: Addressing the Interlinked Challenges of Climate Change, Poverty and Hunger in Asia and the Pacific, provides a stock take of the climate impacts on poverty and food security, and identifies lessons and practices that can tackle their intersection.

The partnership contributes to regional and global policy dialogue, hosting events at ESCAP's annual subregional forums, the Asia-Pacific Forum on Sustainable Development, and the High-level Political Forum on Sustainable Development, the central United Nations platform for the follow-up and review of the SDGs. The partnership also supports a data portal which informs the annual ESCAP report on SDG progress in the region.

Source: Asian Development Bank.

To enable the finance sector in DMCs to support the implementation of the SDG agenda, the regional technical assistance program Leveraging Financial Markets and Instruments for Meeting the SDGs 2021–2024 has been providing advisory support on policy reforms, developing a regulatory environment, and unlocking innovative financing and technology solutions.

Advisory support on SDG implementation at the subnational level

It is estimated that 65% of the 169 targets underlying the 17 SDGs will not be reached without proper engagement with subnational governments.[68] Over the years, ADB has supported several initiatives to promote SDG localization at the subnational level, and the bank's work assisting subnational governments deliver essential public services remains critical.

ADB's e-learning program on SDG localization has completed three editions and the course materials were used as basis for ADB's book entitled Decentralization, Local Governance, and Localizing SDGs in Asia and the Pacific.[69] Additionally, using the conceptual framework of the SDG Country Implementation Snapshots developed by ADB and UNDP, SDG snapshots were also developed at the subnational level. An SDG snapshot at Subnational Administration Level in Indonesia has been developed and a snapshot for Cambodia is forthcoming.

Also in Indonesia, supported by ADB and United Cities and Local Governments Asia-Pacific, the development of the 2021 DKI Jakarta SDGs Voluntary Local Review report contains achievements and a holistic picture of the progress of SDG implementation in DKI Jakarta Province with a focus on good practices carried out by all stakeholders in attaining the SDGs.[70] In February 2024, the Nusantara SDGs Voluntary Local Review Baseline Report was also developed with ADB's assistance to support the Nusantara Capital Authority to integrate SDGs into city development, highlighting achievements in affordable and essential infrastructure.[71]

---

68 OECD and ADB. 2023. Multi-level Governance and Subnational Finance in Asia and the Pacific. OECD Regional Development Papers. No. 61. Paris.

69 ADB. 2022. *Decentralization, Local Governance, and Localizing the Sustainable Development Goals in Asia and the Pacific.* Manila.

70 Daerah Khusus Ibukota Jakarta: Special Capital Region of Jakarta

71 ADB. 2024. *ADB Indonesia Launch SDGs Baseline Report for New Capital City.* News from Country Offices. 22 February. Manila.

SDG data initiatives supported by ADB

To fully implement, plan, and monitor progress on the SDGs, accurate and timely data are key. Only 27 of ADB's 41 DMCs have 50% sufficient data to measure progress toward the SDGs.[72] Recognizing this gap and the importance of data to support SDG progress, ADB helps the region through SDG data generation and monitoring.

Since 2016, ADB's central statistical database, ADB Key Indicators Database, and the annual publication Key Indicators for Asia and the Pacific, have included a focus on SDG progress. The database is available online, enabling easy access to SDG data within member economies and comparisons of SDG progress across countries. ADB's Basic Statistics Series is another annual publication that presents data on development indicators tracking progress toward the SDGs.

As part of the Asia–Pacific SDG Partnership (Box 10), ADB supports the SDG Data Portal to promote and enhance SDG data monitoring. The portal allows the use of more than 1,000 datasets and provides the basis for ESCAP's Asia–Pacific SDG Progress Report.[73] Additionally, the Practical Guidebook on Data Disaggregation for the Sustainable Development Goals, published in May 2021, produced granular and disaggregated data for enhanced SDG monitoring.

The regional technical assistance program Development of New Statistical Resources and Building Capacity in New Data Sources and Technologies, financed on a grant basis by the Government of Japan Fund for Poverty Reduction and administered by ADB, facilitates better monitoring of the SDGs and is currently covering Indonesia and Maldives, and has previously carried out work in the Philippines and Thailand.

Currently, ADB is the regional coordinator for the Asia and Pacific component of the 2021 International Comparison Program (ICP) cycle aimed at producing regional and global purchasing power parities—covering 21 regional economies comprising more than half of the world's population. The ICP is the world's largest statistical initiative under the auspices of the UN Statistical Commission that produces purchasing power parities data.[74]

ADB and UN Women have a partnership (2022–2027) to strengthen gender data and statistics to track and monitor the SDGs, with a focus on SDG 5 targets, and aim to promote gender-responsive governance tools and value chains, support women's entrepreneurship, tackle gender-based violence, and advance knowledge on gender and climate change.

ADB's Knowledge Management Action Plan, published in 2021, recognizes the importance of knowledge to help identify where the bank can add most value in supporting DMCs achieve the SDGs.

72 ESCAP. SDG Data Availability: SDG Gateway (accessed 18 April 2024).

73 ESCAP. 2024. *Asia and the Pacific SDG progress report 2024: showcasing transformative actions.* Bangkok.

74 Purchasing power parity of a currency unit with respect to a reference currency (US dollar is commonly used) represents the number of units of currency of a country required to buy what one US dollar can buy in the United States.

V. Opportunities to Accelerate SDG Progress

Having crossed the halfway point to 2030, more needs to be done to reignite and accelerate the regional transformations that will have a global impact on the SDGs. The remaining years to 2030 present an opportunity to do things differently and implement integrated solutions that speed up progress toward the Goals. Some key opportunities for ADB to step up support include:

MDB Evolution and internal reforms. Leveraging its new operating model, and driven by the global call for MDB Evolution, ADB has an opportunity to innovate and drive SDG solutions at the intersection of sectors and themes and promote holistic approaches to development challenges. ADB's organizational restructuring, combined with increased lending capabilities as a result of capital adequacy reforms in 2023, will provide ADB with an opportunity to increase the effectiveness of its support to DMCs in achieving their development objectives. ADB's Strategy 2030 Midterm review also provides an opportunity to refine the bank's priorities for the future and align them with SDG gaps. The revision of ADB's performance indicators in the new corporate results framework for 2025–2030 will ensure that these new priorities are monitored effectively in support of the SDGs.

Stepping up as Asia and the Pacific's climate bank. With climate action the only SDG that continues to regress, stepping up as Asia and the Pacific's climate bank and raising its climate ambition to $100 billion of its own financing delivered by 2030, ADB is demonstrating its commitment to support the region in addressing the pressing climate crisis. Placing climate action at the forefront, and with the new ADB Climate Change Action Plan requiring all projects to be looked at through a climate lens, the bank has the opportunity to deliver integrated solutions that can reduce the impacts of climate change on poverty and hunger in the region. A strong focus on a just transition has the potential to drive effective transformational change to ensure ADB leaves no one behind. Some promising areas that have been identified are approaches that synergize sustainable development projects with decent work, just transitions, and responsive and adaptive social protection systems (footnote 4).

Facilitating regional cooperation. Many of the dimensions of the SDGs are transboundary in nature, and the crises the region is facing, such as climate change, cannot be addressed by individual countries. ADB is in a strong position to facilitate regional cooperation among national governments and international organizations to address cross-boundary challenges and advance the SDGs agenda collectively. Addressing these common challenges requires the delivery of global and regional public goods that benefit all countries involved.

Enhancing financing support. ADB has increased its ability to support DMCs as a result of the recent capital adequacy reforms, with the additional financing headroom estimated to be $10 billion per year, or $100 billion over the next decade. ADB can continue to bolster its low-cost and patient long-term lending capabilities, including concessional finance. Concessional finance serves as a crucial tool in aiding countries that struggle to access affordable capital. The ADF 14 replenishment in 2024 underscores ADB's commitment to supporting the poorest and most vulnerable DMCs in their pursuit of working toward achieving the SDGs. Moreover, ADB can capitalize on this increased capital to leverage and catalyze even greater additional investments and cofinancing from various sources, especially the private sector, whose finance is critical for achieving the SDGs.

Mobilizing finance. In the current context of debt overhangs and high interest rates, too little private capital is flowing to developing countries. There is an opportunity to pioneer innovative financing models to attract private sector investment for sustainable development initiatives, including models and mechanisms that utilize the SDGs as a framework for impact. This will involve aligning investment strategies with SDG targets and incorporating impact management mechanisms to ensure transparency and accountability. ADB is in a favorable position to identify and bring to life investable opportunities that address the nexus of development challenges in Asia and the Pacific, thus fostering integrated approaches that help achieve simultaneous progress on multiple SDGs.

Figure 13: ADB's Future Pathways to Accelerate SDG Progress

ADB = Asian Development Bank, MDB = multilateral development bank, SDG = Sustainable Development Goal.

Source: Asian Development Bank.

In conclusion, ADB is in a unique position to drive the regional transformations that are essential for advancing progress on the SDGs with a global impact. With the clock ticking to 2030, the institution will seize every opportunity to innovate, collaborate, and mobilize resources on an unprecedented scale.

ADB has made enormous contributions to SDG progress in the region, but there is much more that needs to be done to ensure the goals are met. The road map laid out, from aligning operations, reforming its organizational and capital structure, to evolving as the region's climate bank, reflects ADB's commitment to embrace holistic and systemic approaches. Through enhancing regional cooperation and financing support, ADB will continue to be a driving force for developing countries in the region navigating the complexities of sustainable development—looking onward to a more prosperous, inclusive, resilient, and sustainable future.

Women in the energy sector. Yasmin Fatima, a staff of Patuha Geothermal Power Plant in West Java, Indonesia, discusses with her colleague (photo by Fauzan Ijazah).

Today's catch. Children helping out with the fishing net in Gentuma Raya, Gorontalo, Indonesia (photo by Eric Sales).

Contributors

This report was overseen by Tomoyuki Kimura, director general, Strategy, Policy, and Partnerships Department (SPD), Asian Development Bank (ADB) and Lu Shen, director, Results Management and Aid Effectiveness Division, SPD, ADB. It was led by Carla Ferreira, senior results management specialist, with Mercedes Martin, and a core team including Dave Pipon, Charlene Liau, Beini Liu, Aditya Khurana, Sanskruthi Kalyankar, Frank Thomas, and Millicent Q. Pangilinan. The SDGs Working Group and other focal points from across ADB provided invaluable input and review comments. Tom Felix Joehnk edited the report and Charlene Claret led design.

ADB's SDGs Working Group, led by the Results Management and Aid Effectiveness Division of SPD, aims to promote, aims to promote internal engagement with the 2030 Agenda, alignment of operations and knowledge management in support of the Sustainable Development Goals, and identify opportunities to extend tailored assistance to developing member countries to achieve the 2030 Agenda.

"For I know
the plans
I have for you,"
declares the Lord,
plans to prosper you
& not to harm you,
plans to give
you hope and
a future.
Jeremiah 29:11

Welcome To
CAPITOL TIMES MAGAZINE
GET YOUR SUBSCRIPTION
TODAY!
www.capitoltimesmedia.com/magazine-subscription

JOHN 6:35. JESUS SAID, "I AM THE BREAD OF LIFE; WHOEVER COMES TO ME SHALL NOT HUNGER, AND WHOEVER BELIEVES IN ME SHALL NEVER THIRST." ...

Capitol Times Magazine

ISSN - Print: 2998-8004 | Online: 2998-8012

Editor-In-Chief
Anil Anwar

Associate Editors
David Colbert
Katherine Daigle

Magazine Graphic design
By Saba Jenn

Front Cover Photo
By Michael Mota

Additional Photo Credits

1. Michael Mota
2. Canva Pro
3. Gage Skidmore
4. Donald Trump Whitehouse flickr.com/photos/whitehouse45
5. Paradin Security Solutions LLC

Owned by Capitol Times Media LLC. Printed in the United States of America
© All Rights Reserved - 2024

Copyright Disclaimer: Capitol Times Magazine utilizes photos solely for editorial purposes and provides proper credit to the copyright holders.

www.capitoltimesmedia.com

Disclaimer

The views and opinions expressed in the articles or Interviews published in this magazine are solely those of the respective authors and do not necessarily reflect the official policy or position of the Capitol Times magazine, its editors, or its staff. The authors are solely responsible for the content of their articles.

The magazine strives to provide a platform for diverse voices and opinions, and we value the principle of free expression.

The magazine assumes no responsibility or liability for any errors or omissions in the content of the articles. In no event shall the Capitol Times magazine be liable for any special, direct, indirect, or incidental damages.

Furthermore, the inclusion of advertisements or sponsored content in Capitol Times magazine does not constitute an endorsement or guarantee of the products, services, or views promoted by the advertisers. Readers are encouraged to conduct their own research and exercise caution when making decisions based on advertisements or sponsored content featured in this publication.

Thank you for reading and engaging with our publication. Your feedback is valuable to us as we continue to provide a platform for thought-provoking content and diverse perspectives.

ATTENTION ADVERTISERS AND SPONSORS!

Capitol Times magazine is on the lookout for partners who share our commitment to truth and the promotion of Christian Conservative values. As a trusted publication in the United States, we strive to uphold the highest standards of journalism while championing principles that resonate with our readership.

By advertising with us, you not only gain access to our loyal audience but also align your brand with a publication that stands firm in its dedication to integrity and authenticity. Your support will enable us to continue delivering insightful content that informs, educates, and inspires.

Join us in our mission to make a difference in the world of media. Contact us today to explore advertising and sponsorship opportunities with Capitol Times magazine. Together, let's amplify the voice of conservatism and uphold the values that matter most.

Editor's Note

A Visionary in Action—Michael Mota

In this issue of Capitol Times Magazine, we are honored to feature an exclusive interview with Michael Mota, an entrepreneur whose vision and leadership have transformed multiple industries. From his roots in education, with a B.A. from Rhode Island College and an M.A. in Administration from Providence College, to his impressive work in media, real estate, and entertainment, Michael brings a rare combination of creativity, education, and leadership to all his endeavors.

Perhaps most notably, Michael's entrepreneurial spirit shines through as the founder and CEO of Virtual365. His brainchild, SopranosCon, attracted over 15,000 fans of The Sopranos—a testament to his ability to create unforgettable experiences. With Virtual365, Michael continues to revolutionize live and virtual events, offering a blend of social interaction and VIP experiences that captivate audiences across the globe.

In this issue, we dive into Michael's journey, his innovative spirit, and his thoughts on leadership in today's ever-changing landscape. We hope you find his story as inspiring as we do.

Enjoy the read!

Anil Anwar

Editor-in-Chief

Review Rating

Thomas S

A must read. Turn off the TV. Sit down and read this. Then read it again.

★★★★★

Julie B

All Americans MUST read! This story is amazing and one every American must know.

★★★★★

Leslie D Keller

Important and great article on Patrick Byrne. Everybody needs to read this.

★★★★★

Review Rating

Martha Boneta

Excellent Magazine featuring Patrick Byrne.
Exceptional journalism and cover story featuring Patrick Byrne!

★★★★★

David Colbert

A Riveting Read: Capitol Times Magazine Unveils the Truth about the Deep State

★★★★★

It reveals shocking details about our intelligence agencies, our election system, and how our intelligence community seeks successful and powerful resources from the private sector to help them achieve objectives. America is in peril from foreign enemies and we must peacefully unite if we want to save our country. Time is running short for us to be successful.

★★★★★

CAPITOL TALK
With Anil Anwar
Monday to Fri
7:15 pm EST
or watch LIVE at www.capitoltimesmedia.com

"

Michael Mota is a good soul who has a drive to succeed and the know-how to do so. He is a freedom loving American who is pursuing the American Dream with boundless energy. What are his down sides? There are none that count. His ethics and concern for doing things properly, legally, and ethically are top tier. Perhaps, he isn't as refined as the elite, and can sound a little rough around the edges, but those are just affects of his warm and approachable personality, while his character is founded on ethics of being kind, generous, and productive. Michael lucked out in life, as he was able to watch and learn how to build a business and copy what he learned to advance. So, with Michael, we have a wonderful guy who is successful and growing to achieve what can be achieved only in America.

However, this is not all without problems. Just like any entrepreneur, Michael has had his challenges as well as his successes. Some are simply the little issues which every entrepreneur encounters, some are the exceptional problems of building housing for the unfortunate, and then, on top of everything, one is the problem of having an amateur sleuth who somehow wrangled a job for herself at the Boston Globe who let her off her leash to take a bite out of the success of whichever victim she, in her WOK mentality determined was a worthy target. This is how I got to know this wonderful man, whose only crime is being a conservative. However, to use the words of Abraham Lincoln, this too shall pass.

"

~ Peter Ticktin

Exclusive Interview

Michael Mota

ANIL: *We are honored to sit down with Michael Mota, an entrepreneur and visionary whose diverse expertise spans multiple industries. Michael has built his agency on a solid foundation of education, creativity, and leadership. With a B.A. in Education from Rhode Island College and an M.A. in Administration from Providence College, Michael's background as an educator and videographer adds depth to his work in the world of media and entrepreneurship.*

Michael's entrepreneurial spirit is further showcased through his work as the founder and CEO of Virtual365, where he delivered the widely acclaimed SopranosCon—an event that attracted over 15,000 Sopranos fans. His platform for live and virtual events continues to revolutionize how audiences experience entertainment, offering a seamless blend of social interaction and VIP experiences. With his multi-faceted approach to business and innovation, Michael Mota is a leader who thrives in bringing visionary projects to life, and we are thrilled to dive deeper into his journey and insights in this exclusive interview.

MICHAEL: Thank you, Anil, for the splendid introduction.

ANIL: We know you're the son of immigrants who came to the U.S. in search of a better life. Can you share more about your family background and what your childhood was like growing up?

MICHAEL: I was born and raised in Rhode Island, the smallest state in the nation. My parents are legal immigrants who came here from Portugal when they were only 13 and 14 years old, respectively. Like many others, they came to the United States in search of the American Dream.

They arrived with no money and unable to speak English, but their strong work ethic allowed them to succeed, and they eventually learned the language. They taught my sister and me that to achieve anything in life, you must work hard. I went to school in North Providence, and after college, I returned to teach elementary school.

Currently, I live about a mile away from my childhood home in Lincoln, Rhode Island. I have an amazing wife named Jodi and two wonderful children—Lola (6 years old) and Michael (14 years old).

ANIL: Mr. Mota, you've become an inspirational entrepreneur, and your career began in education. Can you tell us about your early teaching positions and why you left the field to pursue your current path?

MICHAEL: I graduated from high school and attended Rhode Island College, where I earned a Bachelor's Degree in Elementary Education. I began my career as a 3rd-grade teacher for a few years, but I quickly realized I wanted to become a principal. I then went to Providence College and earned my Master's Degree in Administration. While completing my degree, I taught 5th grade for a few more years. During this time, I convinced a friend to run for Congress, and he asked me to manage his campaign. We came in second, which was incredible, considering he was a newcomer to politics. Afterward, he founded a media company and asked me to become Vice President—being a teacher or principal was no longer on my radar. Life often takes you in unexpected directions, and I fell in love with marketing, which became my new path.

ANIL: Can you share more about your time at MediaPeel, which later became Seven Swords Media? How did that experience influence the direction of your career?

MICHAEL: After running my friend's campaign, I became the Vice President of MediaPeel, a full-service advertising and PR agency. I led the team and brought on a large client that was just starting to take off, named Alex and Ani. In their first year, I helped grow their sales from a million dollars to around 75 million. At that point, I knew my future would be in helping Alex and Ani become a billion-dollar company. I facilitated an acquisition where Alex and Ani acquired MediaPeel, making it their official marketing company. We then launched a marketing arm called Seven Swords, which served as the advertising agency for all of Alex and Ani's largest brands. This is how I helped them grow from a million in sales and 20 employees to a billion dollars and a thousand employees.

ANIL: What inspired you to create ATOM Media? Have you achieved the initial goals you set out to accomplish during that company's creation?

MICHAEL: After the CEO of Alex and Ani left for a new position, I decided to leave the company as well and open my own marketing firm. I named it ATOM Media Group for two reasons: 'Atom' is 'Mota' spelled backwards, and everything starts with a single atom. I launched the agency and secured clients such as The Smithsonian in Washington, D.C., Benjamin Moore, Paint Worldwide, and other companies I had worked with during my time at Alex and Ani. I grew the company to 35 employees, and we became a full-service agency. Around that time, I was approached about purchasing a distressed restaurant. I transformed it into a weddings and events venue called Skyline at Waterplace. I focused heavily on promoting and growing it into one of the premier wedding and event spaces in New England. I applied the tools and knowledge I gained during my tenure at Alex and Ani to help my clients moving forward.

ANIL: ATOM Media is reaching its 10th anniversary. What are you currently planning?

MICHAEL: In marketing, you can do one of two things: you can advertise and help other companies grow, or you can focus those same efforts on growing your own company. For our 10th anniversary, we are using our marketing resources to promote our own brands, such as Skyline at Waterplace and Virtual365.

VIRTUAL365 is now a 24/7 'for the fans, by the fans' app that integrates our cryptocurrency, Virtualcoin. It has hosted events like SopranosCon in 2019 (which drew 15,000 attendees and received worldwide coverage) and Mob Movie Con (which featured the first-ever Mob Movie Awards, hosted by Justina Valentine and Ice-T).

We're looking to continue expanding our portfolio by incorporating real estate and helping other businesses grow by applying everything we've learned throughout the years.

ANIL: Your work at Skyline at Waterplace happened during the height of the COVID pandemic. How did you navigate such an unprecedented challenge?

MICHAEL: COVID hit at a time when we were focusing all our efforts on large-scale events like SopranosCon, weddings, and corporate gatherings. COVID brought everything and everyone to a standstill, forcing us to refocus and rethink how we conducted business. Even today, we continue to feel the effects, as the entire hospitality industry has been deeply impacted.

In response, we developed an app for Virtual365 that allows people from around the world to come together without needing to be in person, understanding that people would feel safer this way. We shifted our focus and created something a bit different. The world will certainly never be the same.

ANIL: We understand you're currently suing the Boston Globe for defamation. Can you walk us through how this all started?

MICHAEL: During my tenure at Alex and Ani, the CEO was attacked by a journalist from a local newspaper. She did everything in her power to slander him, along with anyone associated with his business. She attempted to do the same to me but was unsuccessful. Seven years later, during a time when everything was going well for me, she resurfaced under a different newspaper. Given the times we live in, she fabricated events that never occurred and wrote scathing articles—17, to be exact—in the Boston Globe about me and how I run my businesses. This severely undermined all my hard work and efforts and had a significant impact on my businesses and everything I did.

However, I did not stop. Just as I haven't stopped in the past when challenges came my way, I decided to secure a media relations company, TransMedia Group, to help rebuild my brand and reputation (arguably my largest asset) and to bring the truth about me and my businesses to light.

In doing so, we hired Peter Ticktin, a former classmate, friend, and lawyer of Donald Trump, who has extensive experience handling cases of this magnitude and similar to mine. We filed a lawsuit against the Boston Globe, not only for myself but also for my brands, my family, and for all those who lack the means to defend themselves. We're taking action against the Boston Globe to put a stop to these practices.

In 2024, we are living in a world where, unfortunately, it is easy for the media to falsify information and shape it to fit a certain narrative, even when the facts aren't there.

ANIL: Now that the defamation case has been officially filed, have you seen any changes in your professional or personal relationships?

MICHAEL: When the Boston Globe decided to attack me, it made my life difficult. We live in a world where people often judge guilt or innocence based on online articles. Unfortunately, due to the power of the Boston Globe, their articles appear first. People don't see the great things I've done; instead, they see one reporter's slanderous attacks on my personal character. The first thing businesses, investors, and hedge funds do is search your name online. By filing a lawsuit, I'm finally able to counteract these stories and present my side of the situation. For too long, people have only had access to the Boston Globe's fictitious narratives and not the other side of the story. Now that my side is out there, I can use my marketing expertise to share the truth. While I may not have the Boston Globe's reach (which has significantly declined in recent years), I can still reach a global audience by leveraging over 20 years of experience and partnering with the best in the field. People will hear the truth, and I believe that others who have been affected by one-sided media, such as former President Donald Trump, will understand the importance of controlling your own narrative. Don't allow a for-profit company to profit from tearing you down.

ANIL: Your first convention was for the Sopranos fanbase, entitled SopranosCon. Why did you pick this series? How did that convention come together? What did you learn from the experience that you have carried over into other aspects of your profession?

Photo Source: imdb.com

MICHAEL: The Sopranos is my favorite television series for multiple reasons. I believe it was the best-filmed, best-cast, and best-scripted show of all time. It had a huge impact on how shows are portrayed today. Over the years, I've had the privilege of meeting and befriending many cast members from The Sopranos. It only made sense for me to host the first Sopranos event, which I called 'A Night With The Sopranos,' at my venue, Skyline at Waterplace. With millions of fans around the world, the event easily sold out. I had the privilege of a lifetime serving as the MC for four Sopranos cast members.

When we posted photos of the event, I was approached by a fan who had his own social media group with millions of followers. He was blown away by the event and asked if I'd be interested in hosting a smaller event for his followers. I agreed, but on one condition: we would create the biggest event in history. And that's exactly what we did. We hosted it in New Jersey at the Meadowlands Convention Center. We had over 55 Sopranos cast members, Alabama 3 (who performed the theme song featured in every episode) flew in from London, and we had over 15,000 attendees over a two-day period. It was an incredibly immersive event, complete with sets based on the show. It was an experience unlike anything done before.

SopranosCon was featured on The Tonight Show Starring Jimmy Fallon and on hundreds of media networks around the world. It was the first of many events of its kind. When the pandemic slowed down, we held Mob Movie Con, which featured The Sopranos as well as other mob movies (one of the biggest genres in film history). The goal was to bring like-minded individuals together at an event where they could meet others who shared the same passion. We had attendees from all over the world. We will continue to pursue this vision of bringing such events to the public.

If I were to host another event like SopranosCon, it would either focus on TV and film or be centered around boxing. However, these events would be conducted through our app, Virtual365. We also have our own Virtualcoin, which will allow people to experience events all over the world using our technology.

ANIL: Shifting to politics, what are your thoughts on the current political climate in the United States?

MICHAEL: We live in very dangerous times. There are wars happening, open borders allowing millions to come in, rising prices preventing people from buying groceries, and children aspiring to become OnlyFans models and YouTubers instead of doctors and lawyers. We need to change our trajectory and return to what made America great.

It's no secret that I am a Republican and a fan of Donald Trump, but I am also an independent thinker. We need to support change in this next election—if we don't, America won't be the country my parents came to in order to fulfill the American Dream. I blame the media for how they present information, and I blame people who believe everything they read without doing proper research. People need to invest the time to understand they are being led like sheep. In a world of sheep, you must be the shepherd. You must question and research everything and be an independent thinker. If not, the nation will cease to exist.

ANIL: Which well-known individuals inspire you, whether in business, politics, or in terms of personal values?

MICHAEL: First and foremost, I am inspired by my children and my wife. I love seeing my children challenge themselves in life and grow into unique individuals.

PRAYER FOR

ISRAEL

"WHOEVER BLESSES ISRAEL WILL BE BLESSED, AND WHOEVER CURSES ISRAEL WILL BE CURSED."

GENESIS 12:3

I've held many jobs and titles, but the best title is 'Dad.' My wife has stood by my side through all the false headlines and social media posts. She continues to walk with me through this crazy life and helps raise our two beautiful children.

I also look up to former President Donald Trump. Succeeding in the business world is very difficult, and to achieve the levels of success he has, not only in business but also as a personal brand, is incredible. Nobody can take his global brand away from him. He has faced constant attacks from people trying to bring him down, with the focus always on the negatives rather than the positives. He also survived an assassination attempt, and when he was shot, the first thing he did was stand up and reassure people that we would be okay. In the business world, you're often attacked for what you stand for and for your success. For that reason, he inspires me to push through every day.

ANIL: Mr. Mota, before we conclude, we often ask our guests to share their thoughts on Capitol Times Magazine and how endorsements like yours help uphold conservative, Christian Judeo values, and promote free speech. How do you see platforms like ours contributing to the broader mission of preserving these principles in today's cultural and political landscape?

MICHAEL: I think in this new age of media, it is crucial to have platforms like Capitol Times. Our world needs platforms that can counterbalance those that are one-sided and push a specific narrative. It is important to have a space for those with similar views, providing an outlet where their voices can be heard while protecting freedom of speech. There's a big difference between freedom of speech and lies, but unfortunately, those lines have been blurred.

I'm thankful to Capitol Times and Anil Anwar, Editor-in-Chief of Capitol Times Magazine, for allowing me to share my story and for giving me a platform to help people understand who I am and what I stand for.

DONALD TRUMP:

THE LEADER AMERICA NEEDS AGAIN IN 2024

By Anil Anwar
Editor-In-Chief

As we approach the pivotal 2024 presidential election, America stands at a crossroads. The challenges facing our great nation—rising crime, economic instability, unchecked immigration, and a growing loss of faith in our institutions—require bold leadership. In this moment of national uncertainty, one leader stands out for his proven record, his unwavering commitment to American values, and his vision to restore greatness: Donald J. Trump.
Donald Trump isn't just running for president again—he's running to take back the country we love from those who have weakened it. After four years of Joe Biden's failed policies, it's clear that America needs the strength, resolve, and courage that only Trump can provide. His return to the White House is not just a campaign; it's a movement to restore American greatness, security, and prosperity.

A Proven Record of Success

When Donald Trump first took office in 2016, he inherited a nation that had been weakened by years of bad deals, overregulation, and globalist policies. But Trump wasted no time turning things around. His achievements as president speak for themselves:

- **Economic Growth:** Before the COVID-19 pandemic, Trump presided over one of the strongest economies in American history. His tax cuts, deregulation, and pro-business policies created millions of jobs, raised wages, and delivered historic low unemployment rates—particularly among African Americans, Hispanic Americans, and women. Trump's "America First" policies put American workers and businesses first, bringing manufacturing jobs back to the U.S. and standing up to unfair trade practices.

- **Securing Our Borders:** Trump's strong stance on immigration set him apart from any other leader. He delivered on his promise to build the border wall, securing hundreds of miles along the U.S.-Mexico border and dramatically reducing illegal immigration. Trump fought tirelessly to enforce our immigration laws, end sanctuary cities, and protect American citizens from the dangers posed by unchecked immigration.

- **Standing Strong Against Our Enemies:** Trump rebuilt the military and made America respected on the global stage once again. From defeating ISIS to standing up to China's unfair trade practices, Trump showed that he wasn't afraid to challenge America's adversaries. His strong leadership fostered peace in the Middle East with the historic Abraham Accords, achieving what previous administrations had deemed impossible.

- **Law and Order:** Trump understood that without law and order, there can be no peace or prosperity. He worked to support law enforcement, combat rising crime, and protect the rights of law-abiding citizens. As violent crime surges under Joe Biden's leadership, Trump's call for tough-on-crime policies and support for police is needed now more than ever.

- **Fighting for the Forgotten:** Throughout his presidency, Trump fought for the forgotten men and women of America. From championing rural communities to standing up for small businesses, Trump's policies benefited everyday Americans, not the elite or special interests. He revitalized the American energy sector, ensuring that the U.S. became energy independent for the first time in decades.

The Biden Disaster: Why We Need Trump Now

In contrast to Trump's remarkable achievements, Joe Biden's presidency has been nothing short of disastrous. From day one, Biden's far-left agenda has weakened America at home and abroad. Under his leadership, inflation has skyrocketed, our southern border has become a crisis zone, and our foreign policy is in disarray. The American people are suffering under Biden's radical policies, and it's clear that we cannot afford another four years of his presidency.

- **Economic Mismanagement:** Biden's reckless spending and high taxes have fueled historic inflation, making it harder for families to make ends meet. Gas prices are soaring, groceries are more expensive than ever, and the American dream is slipping away for millions. Trump's economic plan, rooted in common sense and pro-growth policies, is the only solution to get our economy back on track.

- **Border Crisis:** Under Biden, illegal immigration has surged to unprecedented levels. His open-border policies have invited millions to cross into the U.S. without consequence, straining resources, increasing crime, and endangering American lives. Trump's commitment to finishing the wall and enforcing immigration laws is critical to restoring order and protecting our borders.

- **Crime Wave:** Biden's weak stance on crime has emboldened criminals, leading to a national crime wave that threatens the safety of every American. Violent crime is on the rise, cities are becoming more dangerous, and the "defund the police" movement has left law enforcement demoralized. Trump's law-and-order message is exactly what America needs to restore safety in our communities.

- **Weak Leadership on the World Stage:** Biden's failures in foreign policy—most notably his disastrous withdrawal from Afghanistan—have emboldened our enemies and diminished America's standing in the world. From China's growing influence to Russia's aggression, the world is less safe under Biden's leadership. Trump's strong, decisive leadership is needed to restore America's position as a global leader.

The Future with Trump: Making America Great Again

Donald Trump's vision for America in 2024 is clear: a nation that is strong, prosperous, and free. His policies will put America back on the path to greatness:

- **Economic Revival:** Trump will implement policies that promote job creation, lower taxes, and cut regulations that stifle growth. His pro-energy policies will ensure that America is once again energy independent, reducing gas prices and strengthening our economy.

- **Border Security:** Trump has vowed to oversee the largest deportation operation in American history, ensuring that our immigration laws are enforced and our borders are secure. He will complete the border wall and stop the flow of illegal immigrants, drugs, and human trafficking into our country.

- **Law and Order:** Trump will restore law and order by supporting law enforcement and implementing tough-on-crime policies. He will ensure that every American can feel safe in their communities, free from the threat of violent crime.

- **Restoring American Pride:** Trump will fight to protect our values, defend our freedoms, and restore pride in our nation. He understands that America is an exceptional nation, and he will work to ensure that future generations inherit a country they can be proud of.

Why Trump Deserves Your Vote in 2024

America is at a tipping point. The radical left has taken control of the Democratic Party and is pushing policies that are destroying America. Joe Biden's presidency has been a disaster, and the consequences of his failed leadership are being felt in every corner of the nation. Now more than ever, we need a strong leader who will put America first.

Donald Trump has proven that he is that leader. His record speaks for itself, and his vision for the future is exactly what America needs to overcome the challenges we face. By voting for Trump in 2024, you're voting for a safer, stronger, and more prosperous America.

This election is about more than politics—it's about the future of America. Make the choice for freedom, security, and prosperity. Make the choice for Donald J. Trump.

America's best days are still ahead, and with Trump back in the White House, Donald Trump will Make America Great Again, Again.

PATRICK BYRNE'S ADVICE TO TRUMP:
ASSEMBLE A WAR CABINET WITH GENERAL FLYNN

By Anil Anwar
Editor-In-Chief

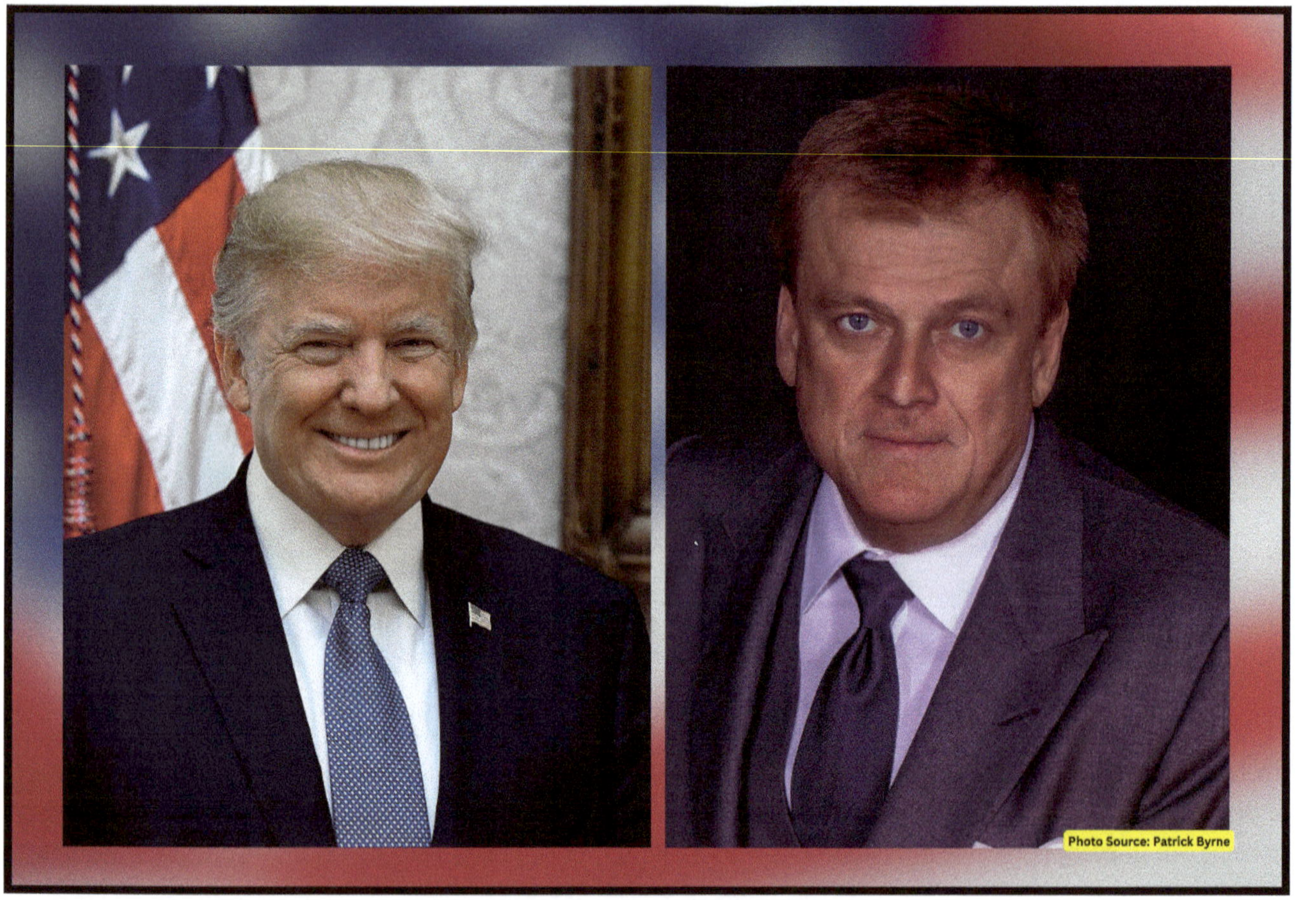

Photo Source: Patrick Byrne

In a powerful and pointed message on X (formerly Twitter), Patrick Byrne, the outspoken businessman and Trump wellwisher, delivered some candid advice to former President Donald J. Trump. Byrne's message was clear: Trump is in a battle for the future of America, and he needs to surround himself with warriors, not mediocrity.

"

You are at war. You need a war cabinet. You need @GenFlynn at your side. Most of the people around you now are mediocre, and some of them don't even want you to win. You should have listened to me December 18, 2020. Listen to me now

Patrick Byrne

"You are at war. You need a war cabinet," Byrne wrote in his post, addressing Trump directly. "You need @GenFlynn at your side."

Patrick Byrne
@PatrickByrne · Follow

Message to @realDonaldTrump :

You are at war.
You need a war cabinet.
You need @GenFlynn at your side.

Most of the people around you now are mediocre, and some of them don't even want you to win.

You should have listened to me December 18, 2020. Listen to me now

1:38 AM · Sep 16, 2024

Byrne, the former CEO of Overstock.com, has long been a vocal advocate for Trump and his fight against the corrupt establishment. His call for Trump to bring in General Michael Flynn—a patriot and military strategist who was one of Trump's closest allies during his presidency—signals the need for strong leadership in this critical moment.

In his latest post, Byrne pointedly reminded Trump that he had offered similar counsel in December 2020, advice he believes the president should have heeded back then. "You should have listened to me December 18, 2020. Listen to me now," Byrne added.

Byrne's message also carried a warning. "Most of the people around you now are mediocre, and some of them don't even want you to win," he stated bluntly. This sentiment will resonate with many Trump supporters who have watched in frustration as establishment figures and lukewarm advisers have failed to stand by Trump's bold America First agenda.

It's no secret that Trump has faced internal opposition from weak or self-interested advisors throughout his political career. Many within his own orbit, particularly during the tumultuous post-election period in 2020, worked against the president's interests.

Byrne's post also carried a note of regret. "You should have listened to me December 18, 2020," he said, referencing the critical moments after the 2020 elections. And now, Byrne insists, is the time to listen. He urged Trump to heed his advice and build a team ready to fight back in this war for America's future. General Flynn, with his deep knowledge of national security and his loyalty to Trump's vision, would be the perfect choice to lead that charge.

As Donald Trump continues to campaign for the 2024 presidential race, he faces unprecedented attacks from all sides—the media, the Democrats, the legal system, and even some within his own party. The stakes couldn't be higher. Byrne's call for a "war cabinet" reflects the reality that Trump is not just running a campaign; he is fighting a war for the soul of the nation.

America needs strong, decisive leadership. Trump needs fighters by his side who are committed to winning, not career politicians and advisors more concerned with their own standing than the future of the country.

Patrick Byrne is no stranger to bold action. His willingness to speak truth to power has made him a key figure in the conservative movement, and his advice to Trump is rooted in a clear vision: surround yourself with patriots who are ready to fight and win. General Flynn, with his military expertise and unwavering loyalty to the cause, would be a critical asset in that battle.

As Byrne aptly put it, "Listen to me now." Trump's path to victory in 2024 will require the kind of leadership and strategy that only a war cabinet can provide. With General Flynn by his side and a team of determined patriots, Trump can rise above the noise, fight back against the forces arrayed against him, and reclaim America for the people.

Patrick Byrne's message is a rallying cry for the MAGA movement—and a reminder to Trump that victory is within reach if he chooses the right people to stand beside him in this historic battle.

The time for half-measures and lukewarm loyalty is over. As Byrne said: "You are at war."

Defending Religious Freedom and Protecting Worshipers from Anti-Israel Hate

By Harrison

As conservative Christians, we stand firm in our belief that religious freedom is a cornerstone of American society, rooted in our nation's Judeo-Christian values. The recent opposition by the California chapter of the Council on American-Islamic Relations (CAIR) to a proposal by the L.A. City Council that aims to protect religious institutions, including synagogues, from anti-Israel protests is both alarming and misguided. This proposal, which would create an eight-foot "bubble zone" around synagogues, churches, mosques, and other religious institutions, is not only necessary but essential to ensure that people of faith can worship freely and without fear.

Antisemitism is on the rise, not only in Los Angeles but across the country, and it often masquerades as so-called "anti-Israel" activism. In reality, many of these protests cross the line into outright hate. The June incidents in Los Angeles, where pro-Palestinian activists obstructed the entrances of synagogues, are a chilling reminder of this growing threat. When protesters target synagogues and harass Jewish worshipers, this is not merely a political protest—it is an attack on the religious freedom that we as Christians hold dear.

The Bible calls us to "pray for the peace of Jerusalem" (Psalm 122:6) and to stand with God's chosen people. As Evangelical Christians, we understand that Israel holds a special place in the divine plan, and when Jewish Americans are targeted for their support of Israel, it is an affront to religious freedom itself. The L.A. City Council's proposal to create an eight-foot buffer around religious institutions, including synagogues, is a measured response to this rising tide of antisemitic hatred. It does not prevent free speech; rather, it ensures that worshipers of all faiths can enter their houses of worship without fear of intimidation or obstruction.

The opposition by CAIR to this common-sense proposal raises serious questions. Why would any organization object to a law that protects the rights of religious minorities to worship in peace? The bubble zone law would apply to all religious institutions, including mosques. Yet, instead of standing with fellow people of faith in supporting this measure, CAIR is siding with radical activists whose actions are creating an atmosphere of fear for Jewish communities.

It is particularly troubling that CAIR would oppose a law designed to combat antisemitism, given the recent wave of attacks against synagogues and Jewish businesses across the country. Their stance is a dangerous one, suggesting that political protests against Israel somehow justify the harassment and obstruction of Jewish Americans trying to exercise their right to worship. This is not the America we believe in.

Nihad Awad
Executive director of the Council on American-Islamic Relations

For those of us who value religious liberty, this proposal is not just about defending synagogues or Jewish worshipers—it is about defending the very principles that make America exceptional. Religious freedom, enshrined in the First Amendment, is a non-negotiable right. We believe that every American, whether Christian, Jewish, or Muslim, should have the ability to worship freely without fear of harassment or violence.

The bubble zone proposal protects that right for all faiths, ensuring that no one—regardless of religion—is intimidated by protesters while entering their place of worship. The fact that it also extends to schools and healthcare facilities further demonstrates the importance of protecting vulnerable institutions from obstruction and harassment.

The Biblical Call to Stand with Israel

As Christians, we are called to stand with Israel and the Jewish people. Genesis 12:3 reminds us of the covenant God made with Abraham: "I will bless those who bless you, and whoever curses you I will curse." In the face of rising antisemitism and hatred toward Israel, it is our duty as believers to stand in solidarity with our Jewish brothers and sisters.

The growing hostility toward Israel and the Jewish community in America is not just a political issue—it is a spiritual battle. When protesters attack synagogues and intimidate worshipers, they are attacking the values that underpin our faith. This is why the L.A. City Council's bubble zone proposal is so important: it provides necessary protection to those targeted by hate.

It is time for conservative Evangelicals to make our voices heard on this issue. We cannot sit idly by while religious freedoms are threatened. We must support policies like the bubble zone proposal that safeguard worshipers of all faiths from intimidation and harassment. At a time when antisemitism is on the rise, we must stand boldly with the Jewish community, not just out of political solidarity, but out of our deeply held Christian convictions.

To CAIR and those who oppose this measure, we say: Religious freedom is not negotiable. The right to worship without fear or intimidation is a fundamental American value, and any attempts to undermine that right should be condemned.

As we continue to pray for the peace of Jerusalem, let us also pray for the safety and protection of all who seek to worship freely in America. Now is the time to stand firm in our commitment to religious liberty and to defend those who are being targeted simply for their faith. The bubble zone proposal is a step in the right direction, and it deserves the full support of all Americans who cherish freedom.

Trump's Bold Stand for American Sovereignty and Security in Springfield

By Saba Jenn

Donald Trump has never been one to shy away from addressing the hard truths facing America as a country, and his recent vow to oversee the **"largest deportation in the history of our country"** is yet another example of his commitment to restoring order and protecting American communities. Speaking in Springfield, Ohio, Trump made it clear: the time has come to prioritize the safety, security, and well-being of American citizens over unchecked immigration.

Springfield, a small town of 58,000 residents, has recently found itself at the center of a growing national conversation about immigration, crime, and cultural strife. The town has welcomed nearly 15,000 Haitian immigrants in recent years, an influx that has strained local resources and ignited concerns among longtime residents. Reports of cultural clashes, increases in crime, and a growing welfare crisis have dominated local discourse, and now, following a series of disturbing incidents, the national spotlight is on Springfield.

The shocking case of Allexis Telia Ferrell, who was arrested for allegedly killing and eating a cat in broad daylight, has sent shockwaves through the community. While police have confirmed that Ferrell is a U.S. citizen, the incident underscores the growing unease in Springfield as the town grapples with cultural tensions brought on by rapid changes in demographics.

Conservative journalist Christopher Rufo's report alleging similar incidents in neighboring Dayton adds another layer to this unfolding crisis. While these claims remain unconfirmed, they tap into the fears of many Americans who are witnessing their communities change in ways they never imagined.

Donald Trump's vow to oversee the largest deportation operation in American history is a bold and necessary step to reclaim control of U.S. borders and protect communities like Springfield. For too long, political leaders have turned a blind eye to the cultural and economic strains that unchecked immigration has placed on small towns and cities across the country. Under Joe Biden's administration, these problems have only intensified.

Trump's America First agenda isn't just about protecting U.S. borders—it's about preserving the values, culture, and safety of the American people. Springfield's struggles are emblematic of what happens when the federal government fails to enforce immigration laws and allows waves of migrants to enter the country without adequate vetting or resources to support them.

The influx of Haitian immigrants into Springfield has caused significant strain on the town's welfare system and housing market. Local residents have reported spikes in crime and social discord, and the community is struggling to accommodate the rapid changes brought about by this population boom.

Trump recognizes that communities like Springfield need relief, and that begins with strong immigration enforcement.

As the 2024 election approaches, Americans face a clear choice between two vastly different visions for the future of our country. On one side is Donald Trump, who has proven time and again that he will fight to protect American sovereignty, defend our communities, and restore law and order. On the other side is the Biden-Harris administration, which has championed open borders, sanctuary cities, and policies that prioritize illegal immigrants over law-abiding American citizens.

Trump's pledge to deport those who threaten the safety and security of American neighborhoods isn't just a campaign promise—it's a commitment to the values that built this nation. Springfield, Ohio, is just one example of a community crying out for help, and Trump is the only candidate willing to take the bold action necessary to address the crisis.

Donald Trump's plan to restore order through strong immigration enforcement is the solution Springfield—and America—needs. By securing U.S. borders and deporting those who pose a threat to our communities, Trump is offering a path to renewed safety, economic stability, and cultural cohesion. Springfield's experience serves as a microcosm of the larger issues plaguing our nation, and Trump is the only candidate with the vision and courage to tackle these challenges head-on.

As the 2024 election approaches, the choice couldn't be clearer. America can either continue down the path of lawlessness and unchecked immigration, or it can choose to restore order and protect its citizens. Donald Trump's promise to oversee the largest deportation operation in U.S. history is a bold and necessary step in the right direction, and it's one that will resonate with millions of Americans who are ready to take their country back.

Springfield deserves better—and so does America.

CHRISTIAN TIMES MAGAZINE ENDORESE
DONALD TRUMP

Charles Lingerfelt | Editor-in-Chief, Christian Times Magazine
214-850-1541

SAVE AMERICA:

VOTE DONALD TRUMP

The Only Choice to Protect Our Future

By David Colbert
Associate Editor, Capitol Times Magazine

As we approach one of the most crucial elections in American history, the question is not just about who will lead our country for the next four years; it's about whether we will save America or watch it descend into chaos and socialism. With every passing day, the battle lines are becoming clearer: it's either Donald Trump or a far-left agenda under Kamala Harris that will turn America into a failed socialist state akin to Venezuela.

Trump: A Proven Fighter for America

Donald Trump stands as the last, best hope for preserving the values that have made America the greatest country in the world. His track record speaks for itself. Under his leadership, the U.S. economy surged, unemployment hit record lows, and America reclaimed its position as a leader on the global stage. Trump's America First policy put our citizens first—strengthening our borders, protecting our jobs, and ensuring that the country remained free from oppressive government overreach.

Trump understands the American worker and the importance of keeping American families strong and self-reliant. He knows what it takes to protect the Second Amendment, maintain law and order, and stand up to radical leftists who want to dismantle everything we hold dear.

Kamala Harris: A Threat to American Values

On the other side is Kamala Harris, who represents everything wrong with the current Democratic Party. Harris, a far-left vice president, is more than just a political threat; she embodies the dangerous socialist ideas that have plagued failed states like Venezuela. Under her leadership, America could follow in Venezuela's footsteps—a once prosperous country now devastated by socialist policies that have brought economic collapse, widespread poverty, and rampant crime.

Harris and her radical allies are pushing for a version of America that most of us wouldn't even recognize. Open borders, defunding the police, destroying small businesses with crippling taxes and regulations, and waging war on free speech and religious freedoms—this is what Harris has in store for us.

Let's be clear: the Harris agenda is a recipe for disaster. America under a Harris administration would face economic ruin, much like Venezuela. Her radical plans for Medicare-for-All, the Green New Deal, and massive increases in government control would cripple private industry, destroy jobs, and leave millions dependent on government handouts. Harris would not just weaken America's economy but destroy its very foundation, turning the American dream into a socialist nightmare.

Her disdain for capitalism is a threat to every small business owner, every hard-working American trying to provide for their families. The big government, socialist-style programs she champions would cripple our economic freedoms, limit innovation, and put us on a path to economic decline.

But it's not just the economy that's at risk. Kamala Harris and her far-left backers are also pushing a dangerous agenda of lawlessness and social disorder. Under her administration, the already rampant crime waves in our cities will spiral out of control. The calls to defund the police, something she has endorsed in her own way, will leave our neighborhoods unprotected, our families unsafe, and our communities vulnerable to lawlessness.

We've already seen what happens when far-left policies are enacted. Look at cities like Portland, Seattle, and San Francisco—once thriving communities, now overrun with crime, homelessness, and chaos. That's the future Harris wants for the entire country.

Donald Trump, on the other hand, has always been a steadfast supporter of law and order. He understands that a nation without laws is not a nation at all. Throughout his presidency, Trump defended our brave police officers, secured our borders, and pushed back against those who want to dismantle the very fabric of our society.

On the world stage, Donald Trump restored respect for America. He renegotiated trade deals to benefit American workers, confronted China's unfair trade practices, and ensured that NATO allies pulled their weight.

Trump's foreign policy was about standing strong, showing that America would not be pushed around or taken advantage of.

Kamala Harris, however, would return us to the weak, globalist policies that made America vulnerable. Her administration would appease our enemies and undermine our allies, leaving America exposed on the world stage. A Harris presidency would be a return to the disastrous foreign policies that weakened us under Obama and Biden, and it would jeopardize American security.

This election is about more than just policy; it's about survival. The choice is clear: If you want to save America, vote for Donald Trump. He is the only candidate with the strength, conviction, and vision to lead this nation through these perilous times. Harris represents a dangerous, far-left ideology that will strip America of its greatness and drag us into the kind of socialist nightmare we've seen in places like Venezuela.

There is no middle ground. This election will determine the fate of America and the future of freedom around the world. The stakes could not be higher. Voting for Donald Trump is not just about supporting a candidate—it's about preserving the American way of life.

It's about protecting your family, your freedom, and your future.

We cannot afford to experiment with radical socialism. We cannot allow America to fall into the hands of the far-left. Now is the time to take a stand and ensure that we continue to live in a country where freedom, opportunity, and prosperity reign.

Make the Right Choice: Vote Donald Trump.
Save America. Save the World.

VOTE

DONALD TRUMP

Subscribe today to gain exclusive access to in-depth analysis, thought-provoking commentary, and expert opinions. Stay informed and engaged with the latest developments shaping our nation and world.

Subscribe now to Capitol Times Magazine and elevate your understanding of conservative principles and ideologies.

SUBSCRIBE TODAY AND GET STARTED!

www.capitoltimesmedia.com/magazine-subscription

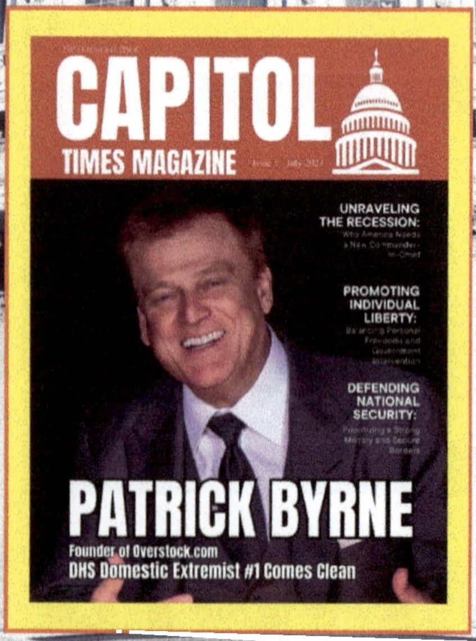

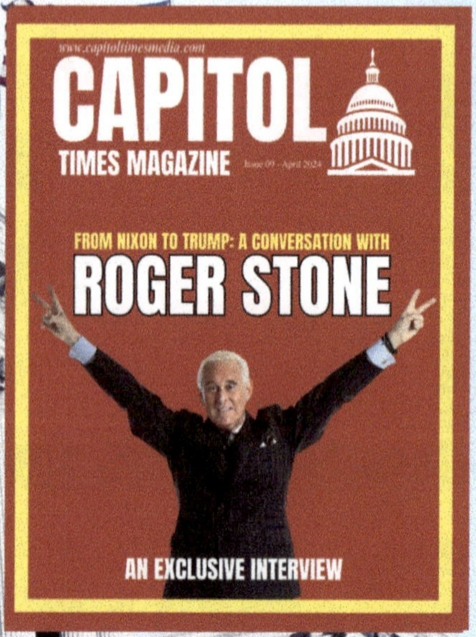

KAMALA HARRIS' RADICAL PROGRESSIVE AGENDA: A THREAT TO FAITH, FAMILY, AND FREEDOM

By Suneel Anwar

As Vice President Kamala Harris gears up for the 2024 election, her resurfaced positions from 2019 reveal a progressive agenda that should alarm every evangelical, conservative, and freedom-loving American. According to a recent CNN report, Harris, in a 2019 questionnaire from the American Civil Liberties Union (ACLU), supported radical policies such as taxpayer-funded gender-transition surgeries for detained immigrants and federal prisoners. This alone should give any God-fearing American pause as it signifies a troubling direction for the moral and ethical compass of our nation.

Kamala Harris' advocacy for taxpayer-funded gender-transition surgeries represents an alarming departure from the Judeo-Christian values that have sustained America. Gender ideology has become a battleground in the cultural war for the soul of our nation. Harris' support for these surgeries—funded by hard-working Americans —signals a growing disregard for the sanctity of God's creation.

Scripture reminds us that we are "fearfully and wonderfully made" (Psalm 139:14), and gender is part of God's divine design. Yet, under Harris' vision for America, the government would promote the confusion of gender roles, turning a blind eye to the moral consequences of endorsing and facilitating such surgeries for individuals, including detained immigrants and prisoners.

This agenda erodes the traditional family unit, undermines biblical truths, and uses taxpayer dollars to advance a radical social experiment.

Harris' support for defunding ICE and abolishing immigrant detention is another dangerous step toward lawlessness.

The Bible teaches us to respect authority and uphold the law (Romans 13:1-7), but Harris seems intent on dismantling the systems that maintain our safety and security. Without ICE, we would see unchecked illegal immigration, leading to further chaos at the border and in our communities.

In the same ACLU questionnaire, Harris advocated for the decriminalization of federal drug possession by legalizing marijuana. While she frames this policy as treating drug addiction as a public health issue, this proposal is dangerous. Legalizing drugs without addressing the root causes of addiction only leads to further destruction of families and communities. Harris' co-sponsorship of the Marijuana Justice Act reveals her willingness to prioritize progressive ideals over moral responsibility.

During the 2019 Democratic primary debates, then-Representative Tulsi Gabbard criticized Harris for her record on criminal prosecutions related to drug possession. Harris' inconsistent stance on this issue is evident; one moment, she positions herself as tough on crime, and the next, she champions policies that would lead to further drug-related devastation in our neighborhoods. Evangelicals and conservatives know that true compassion means helping people overcome their addictions, not promoting policies that entrench them further in bondage.

Harris' progressive agenda also includes proposals to protect abortion nationwide. This stance is an affront to one of the core tenets of Christian belief: the sanctity of life. Harris has long been a staunch advocate for pro-abortion policies, supporting measures that would allow for the destruction of innocent unborn lives under the guise of "women's rights." Yet, as followers of Christ, we know that life begins at conception, and every unborn child is precious in the eyes of God (Jeremiah 1:5).

Harris' radical policies would make it easier for abortion providers to operate and even receive federal protection. If Harris succeeds, more unborn children will be at risk, and America will continue to drift further from the biblical principles of protecting life.

Kamala Harris' progressive platform presents a grave threat to the future of our nation. Her support for gender-transition surgeries, defunding ICE, decriminalizing drug possession, and advancing pro-abortion policies reveals a dangerous agenda that will lead America down a path of moral decline and societal destruction.

As Christians, evangelicals, conservatives, and patriots, we must stand firm against these radical ideas. America's founding principles—faith, family, and freedom—are under siege, and Harris' platform will only accelerate our nation's decline into a godless, lawless society.

There is only one candidate in the 2024 election who stands for the values that have made America great: Donald Trump. He has consistently defended the sanctity of life, protected our borders, and championed law and order. Trump stands as a bulwark against the radical left and their attempts to dismantle the very foundations of our nation.

This election is not just about politics—it is a fight for the soul of America. We must pray for our country and do everything in our power to preserve the values that honor God.

That begins by rejecting Kamala Harris' radical agenda and voting for Donald Trump.

In this pivotal moment, let us remember 2 Chronicles 7:14: "If my people, who are called by my name, will humble themselves and pray and seek my face and turn from their wicked ways, then I will hear from heaven, and I will forgive their sin and will heal their land." We must turn back to God and vote for leaders who will uphold righteousness and truth.

Vote for Trump. Save America. Protect our future.

STANDING WITH ISRAEL:

DEFENDING A NATION'S RIGHT TO PROTECT ITS PEOPLE

By Rebecca Jackson

Once again, the world's media has chosen to criticize Israel for daring to defend itself in the face of relentless terrorism. In June, Israel undertook a daring preemptive strike to rescue four innocent civilians from the grip of Hamas, a terrorist organization known for its ruthless tactics and disregard for human life. Instead of receiving the recognition and praise it deserved for executing a nearly impossible mission to save lives, Israel was immediately vilified by the mainstream media for "collateral damage" that was exaggerated by Hamas propagandists.

The audacity of the world's press to take the word of a terrorist organization over the heroic actions of Israel Defense Forces (IDF) is a testament to the anti-Israel bias that runs rampant in today's media. While Israel meticulously plans and executes missions with the utmost concern for minimizing civilian casualties, the media blindly repeats the false casualty numbers provided by Hamas, which manipulates public opinion to smear Israel's reputation.

As Christians and conservatives, we recognize Israel's God-given right to defend itself. Scripture tells us to "pray for the peace of Jerusalem" (Psalm 122:6) and to stand with God's chosen people. The nation of Israel is surrounded by enemies, and yet it has consistently upheld its moral duty to protect its citizens—Jewish, Christian, and Arab alike—from the ever-present threat of terrorism.

A Fight Against Evil

Hamas is not just a political entity; it is a terrorist organization that thrives on chaos and violence. Its charter calls for the destruction of Israel and the murder of Jews, and it regularly uses innocent civilians as human shields, placing them in harm's way to generate the very "collateral damage" the media loves to report. When Israel acts to protect its people from these violent extremists, it does so with precision and care, unlike Hamas, which indiscriminately targets civilians.

The mission was a prime example of Israel's commitment to saving lives. Four hostages were rescued alive and unharmed—an achievement that should have been celebrated as a victory for freedom and humanity. Instead, journalists chose to focus on Hamas's false claims of casualties, playing into the hands of the terrorists and ignoring the fact that Israel was forced into action by Hamas's unprovoked aggression.

A Call for Christian Solidarity

As Christians, we must stand unequivocally with Israel. The Jewish people have faced persecution throughout history, and today, they are still surrounded by those who wish to see them wiped off the map. God's covenant with Israel is eternal, and we are called to bless Israel, as ***Genesis 12:3 declares: "I will bless those who bless you, and whoever curses you I will curse."***

Israel's struggle is not only political; it is spiritual. The battle against Hamas and other terrorist groups is a battle between good and evil. Israel stands on the front lines of this battle, not just for its own survival, but for the survival of freedom, democracy, and the rule of law in the Middle East.

Standing Against Media Bias

We must also recognize the dangers of a biased media that consistently holds Israel to impossible moral standards while turning a blind eye to the atrocities committed by Hamas and other radical Islamist groups. Israel is castigated for defending itself, while Hamas is portrayed as a victim, even though it is the very source of violence in the region. The media's credibility is called into question when it blindly accepts Hamas's casualty figures without verification and when it downplays Israel's efforts to minimize civilian harm in its military operations. It is time for the media to stop treating Israel as the aggressor and start recognizing the real threat—terrorism. Israel should be commended for its restraint, its commitment to peace, and its determination to protect innocent lives in the face of evil.

Support Israel, Stand for Truth

As Christians, we have a moral duty to stand with Israel. The attacks against Israel in the media are not just attacks on a nation; they are attacks on truth, justice, and the very principles of freedom that we hold dear. Israel's fight is our fight—against terrorism, against evil, and against the forces that seek to destroy what is good.

Let us pray for the peace of Jerusalem and for the safety of the brave men and women of the IDF who stand in defense of their nation and the free world. And let us continue to speak out boldly in support of Israel, knowing that by doing so, we stand on the side of righteousness.

Now, more than ever, we must stand with Israel, the land of God's chosen people, in its fight against terror and in defense of the freedoms we all hold dear.

John 3:16

LARA TRUMP

Leaving Nothing to Chance

By Katherine Daigle

President Trump’s family has always played a significant role in their fathers’ businesses and some in politics, but today, more than ever, we must stay focused in the Final Battle for our Republic. Since 2016, when President Trump won the White House, and in the years following, his family has enjoyed a prominent role in conservative politics and the media arena, especially during and after President Trump's first administration.

Photo By: Gage Skidmore
www.flickr.com/photos/gageskidmore

President Trump's public image has always been steadfast and in control. As he is a strategist who ensures his values, like family and faith, are readily communicated clearly to the electorate. He tailors his messages to appeal to working families, seniors, and minority communities. Trump is a very direct candidate. There is loyalty and trust that cannot be outsourced especially in politics, I personally know these roles are critical to a candidate's campaign. No one is trusted within the circle more than your family. I see Lara as the perfect embodiment of a Republican Party chairperson, a trusted, honest, business-savvy woman who has held executive roles in a very prominent family politically and as a corporate executive. She is aptly skilled in communications.

Today, we have the Republican party, which is presently amid a bona fide political revolution. Something that never should have been able to happen has happened: An outsider candidate, Donald Trump, is fighting for our nation for a second or third time, and he has handed the communications reigns of his political party to a trusted, loyal, savvy family member, Lara Trump.

President Trump's Daughter-in-Law, Eric Trump's Wife, Mother, and Party Chief: Lara Trump's Dual Roles

President Trump's recommendation was that Lara Lea Trump be named the co-chair of the Republican Party he had hand-picked her for that role as Trump runs for another White House term.

Lara Trump's involvement with the RNC is rooted in her deep connections to the Trump political dynasty. The future of the Republican Party lies with her influence within the true conservative party and is likely to continue growing as she takes on more political and public roles.

Lara Trump, now the co-chair of the Republican Party, and as President Trump stood atop the RNC party apparatus firmly under his grip, the RNC officially elected Donald Trump.

Within a week, Lara Trump declared that "every single penny will go to the number one and the only job of the RNC is to elect Donald J. Trump as president of the United States and save this country." Officially on March 8, 2024, Lara Trump was elected co-chair of the RNC unanimously.

Lara Lea Trump— Lara has since been a prominent campaign surrogate and advocate for Trump's policies. She has been a critical voice in connecting with grassroots supporters, focusing on the concerns of families, women, and everyday Americans. She has played an active role in Donald Trump's presidential campaigns in 2016 and 2020.

Lara Trump was strategic almost immediately to take in millions in donations, which were boosted by MAGA outrage over Trump's conviction of thirty-four felony counts. She has held training sessions nationwide, recruiting the President Trump's faithful to be poll watchers; her goal is to enlist more than 100,000 people in battleground states.

"Lara Trump has the potential to move forward in the MAGA World. As an articulate Trump defender and one of his most prominent surrogates, she would have an extensive list of options should her father-in-law reclaim the White House, ranging from a senior role in a second Trump term to elected office. "If we win," says Charlie Kirk, the right-wing firebrand, "she'll be one of the most sought-after and respected people in the conservative movement."

Lara is known for being closely knit with the family and is highly visible. The whole Trump dynasty often embodies the values of loyalty, hard work, and dedicated support for America's families. The Trump family has been a prominent symbol of the business-oriented, #AmericaFirst image that Trump projected during his first presidency. His family were vital players in both his political and business success. His continued influence within the Republican Party has also been a keystone in building his dynasty.

When a political candidate runs for office especially for President of the United States, voters will gravitate towards core values such as family, faith, and leadership, today's administration severely lacks these traits. These qualities are critical because they reflect the candidate's character, principles, and positive national vision.

"We've come a long way, baby!"

This expression was something folks used to say in the '"70s; it certainly is not an En-vogue expression anymore, but most people still recognize it to mean that things have changed from their original form – that they have covered much ground. The phrase universally applies to the women of America particularly the conservative movement because that certainly has evolved over the past few decades. Of course, saying women had "come a long way" usually carries a connotation of improvement, that we are better off than we were before (one undertakes a long journey to reach a better place, after all).

I must digress after the last four years under the Biden/Harris regime women have been trampled and crushed under this socialist agenda put forth by this administration.

Lara Trump a refreshing change. Lara is wasting no time rebranding the typically dull Republican National Committee in the image of her father-in-law, President Donald Trump, and highlighting her own version of his pugilistic politics and brash management style. A softer touch that will appeal to women and families. "Lara was the producer and host of Trump Productions' Real News Update and a producer of Inside Edition. On March 29, 2021, she joined Fox News as a contributor. In December 2022, however, Fox News announced that it decided to part ways with Lara Trump because it had a policy not to employ anyone running for office or involved with a candidate." (Wikipedia) At one point in her career, it was widely rumored that "Lara would run for the United States Senate seat being vacated by the retiring Richard Burr. However, after several months of media speculation, she declined to run and endorsed the eventual winner. " ("Lara Trump - Wikiwand") (The Right View)

At the Republican National Convention, the whole family played starring roles in the nomination process to solidify President Trump as the candidate for the people. Lara & Eric Trump wife, mother, and co-chair of the Republican Party, walked to the center stage at this year's 2024 Republican National Convention; it was a moment that symbolized a change of guard in the Trump family. Lara Lea the mom of their beautiful two children., took the opportunity to offer voters a second look at her father-in-law's softer edges, centering on his family role as the prominent patriarch and grandfather to her two young children.

The Republican party faithful and devoted crowd roared as Lara raised a fist and spoke about a gunman's attempt on her father-in-law's life that day in Butler, Pennsylvania. The "bullet narrowly missed his head. On that day that you were not sure existed until you saw it with your own eyes," she told the crowd. ("Lara Trump's meteoric rise signals changing of Trump family guard - BBC")

I am happy to see that even in the oppressive climate of today against women athletes, mothers, and privacy, we have real women who show us what #MAGA movement ought to mean. I am talking about people like Melania Trump, Ivanka Trump, and Lara Lea Trump, three actualized and empowered women who control their own lives without feeling the need to be strong and independent of family. Lara is a close adviser and confidant of President Trump, having earned her way into a powerful place in his campaign, managing Trump's campaign brand while participating heavily in her father-in-law's Republican Party and political affairs.

Lara, a wife, and mother of two, balances her father-in-law's presidential campaign, co-chair for the Republican Party, and a vital fundraiser for the Republican Party.

She was the first family member to speak officially at the convention, and her presence has ignited interest in her role in the family and any further political ambitions. "Trump's legal spokesperson Alina "she spoke from the heart. She spoke about moms. She spoke about him being a grandfather - things only she can discuss."

"Long-time observers expect Lara Trump's prominence in the family only to grow. Her speech was her introduction to the nation in a big way because while she's had roles in campaigns previously and while she's been a part of Trump's inner circle and family orbit for the last eight years, this is the first time she is positioned in a role that has real power inside the Republican Party, said

Eric Cortellessa, a reporter who recently interviewed Ms. Trump for a Time magazine profile. And she is in a position where she is out to prove herself as an effective surrogate for Trump and a political operator. And we'll see that play out in the next several months as she's cochairing the RNC." (FirstEyeNews.com)

That is what the conservative movement looks like to me, friends: a powerful, independent woman in control of her own life who loves her femininity and nurtures children responsibly (and quite literally, in the case of the image of her children with Grandpa Trump) with poise balancing her obligations. She is an inspiration, I think, for women everywhere.

A woman, mom, and wife campaigning for a candidate can symbolize how essential family values are to voters. Lara Trump represents the importance of a stable home, hard work, and a sense of duty to the next generation. Her message can resonate deeply with voters, particularly those who prioritize traditional values and see the family unit as the cornerstone of society.
Her campaign for President Trump emphasizes that strong families contribute to strong communities and that her candidate's policies, whether related to God and country, health care, education, and family values are rooted in the belief that they will help families thrive. Lara has highlighted how Trump, her children's grandpa, shares those values and will fight for the future of all families, not just for political power.

By showing how President Trump prioritizes family and understands its challenges, she will inspire trust and unity among voters, reminding them that the well-being of their own families is central to the candidate's mission and today is at stake more than ever before. We all want a better future for our families. We have a mission but a collective one—that by working together, America's voters and their families can ensure that the American Dream remains alive for generations to come.

MAKE
AMERICA
GREAT AGAIN!

A CONSERVATIVE STRONGHOLD IN PRIVATE SECURITY

In an age where security threats loom larger than ever, Paradin Security Solutions LLC stands as a beacon of safety and reliability. Founded in 2020 by seasoned private security experts Ryan Lingerfelt and Johnson Kuruvilla, this pioneering company has swiftly risen to prominence by delivering top-tier security services to high-profile clients, including dignitaries and high-net-worth individuals.

DEFENDING WHAT MATTERS MOST

Paradin's mission aligns seamlessly with core conservative values—personal responsibility, strong defense, and the protection of individual liberty. In a world where law and order are increasingly challenged, Paradin provides its clients with the peace of mind that comes from knowing that their security is in the hands of experts. Ryan and Johnson bring a wealth of experience, having safeguarded some of the most prominent individuals in the world, and their company is built on the same principles that make America strong—discipline, vigilance, and a commitment to excellence.

Their meticulous approach to customer care is a reflection of their belief that every life and every property deserve the utmost protection. In a society where uncertainty seems to be the new normal, Paradin Security Solutions offers a level of safety that goes beyond mere service—it's a promise to stand strong for those who trust them.

A TESTAMENT TO AMERICAN ENTREPRENEURSHIP

Paradin Security Solutions is also a shining example of American entrepreneurship at its finest. Founded during the turbulent year of 2020, Ryan and Johnson took the bold step of creating a company dedicated to one of the most important aspects of freedom: security. Their success is a testament to the belief that private enterprise, guided by strong values and clear vision, can thrive even in the most challenging times.

Paradin's commitment to excellence is not just a business strategy; it's a way of life. This company represents the kind of rugged individualism and entrepreneurial spirit that conservatives admire—building something from the ground up, with an unshakable belief in the power of hard work and integrity.

A Future-Ready Approach

While Paradin's roots are deeply grounded in traditional security practices, the company is also forward-thinking, leveraging the latest technology to provide unparalleled protection. Whether it's state-of-the-art surveillance systems or the use of cutting-edge communication tools, Paradin remains on the front lines of security innovation. This combination of experience and technology ensures that their clients receive the best of both worlds—the knowledge of seasoned professionals paired with the power of modern tools.

Defending Freedom, One Client at a Time

At a time when law enforcement is under attack and personal safety is no longer guaranteed, companies like Paradin Security Solutions are more vital than ever. For those who value their freedom, their property, and their way of life, Paradin offers more than just protection—it offers peace of mind. Ryan Lingerfelt and Johnson Kuruvilla understand the risks their clients face, and their personal commitment to security means they will stop at nothing to ensure that those they protect remain safe.

In a world where freedom and safety are increasingly under threat, Paradin stands firm. Just as conservatives believe in a strong national defense, Paradin Security Solutions embodies the belief that personal security is the foundation of liberty. By trusting Paradin, clients are not just securing their physical safety—they are defending their right to live freely, without fear.

Paradin Security Solutions LLC is more than just a company; it's a symbol of conservative values in action. Founded on the principles of self-reliance, personal responsibility, and a strong commitment to safety, Paradin provides a vital service to those who understand the value of protecting what is most precious. With Ryan Lingerfelt and Johnson Kuruvilla at the helm, Paradin stands as a pillar of strength in an uncertain world, reminding us all that freedom requires vigilance, and that true security begins with the courage to take control of our own destiny.

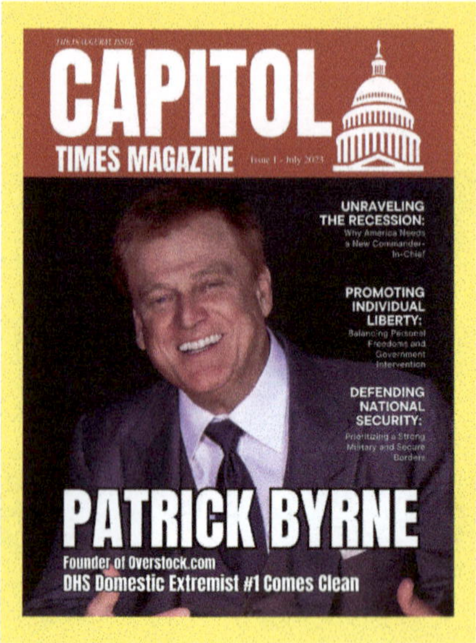

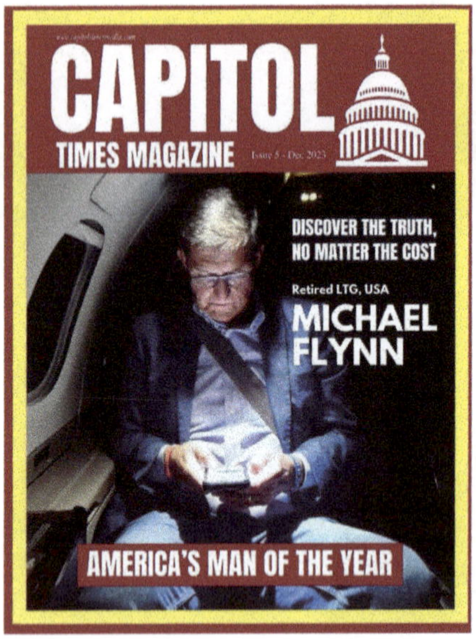

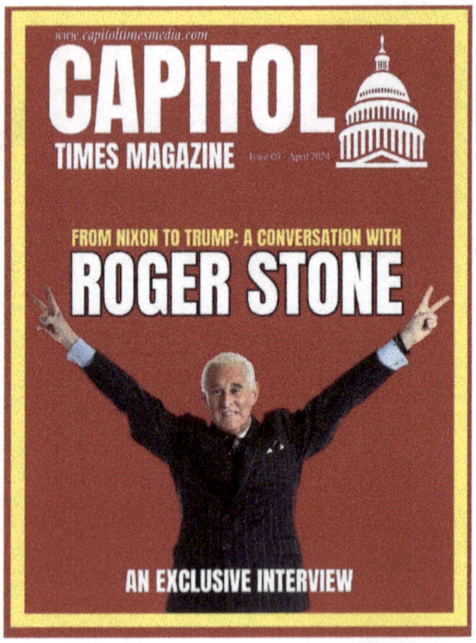

CAPITOL TIMES MAGAZINE:

A VOICE FOR CONSERVATIVE VALUES

In a time when traditional values are being tested like never before, Capitol Times Magazine proudly stands as a beacon for conservative ideals, faith, and freedom. As the most prominent conservative publication in the United States, we are dedicated to upholding the principles that make our nation strong—faith in God, the sanctity of life, limited government, and a free market that fosters opportunity for all.

Over the year, Capitol Times Magazine has become a trusted voice for thousands of conservative Americans, providing honest journalism, insightful commentary, and a platform for the voices that mainstream media often silences.

Our commitment to "No Censorship" is unwavering, and we refuse to bow to the pressures of cancel culture or shadow bans on social media.

We've faced restrictions, but by the grace of God and the support of readers like you, we continue to grow and stand tall.

We Need Your Support: Keep Conservative Media Strong

The mission of Capitol Times Magazine is clear: to provide a platform for conservative, Christian, and family-centered values. But maintaining a strong, independent voice in today's world is no easy task. We are calling on you—our readers, our fellow believers, and patriotic Americans—to help us continue this fight for freedom.

Here's how you can support us:

1. **Subscribe and Share:** By subscribing to Capitol Times Magazine, you're not just receiving the best in conservative commentary; you're also supporting a media outlet that won't compromise on truth. Share our articles, tell your friends, and get others to join our community of patriots.
2. **Donate to the Cause:** Your financial contributions go a long way in helping us resist the pressures from big tech and liberal media outlets. Every dollar you donate helps us continue to publish articles that matter, fight for Christian values, and keep America free.
3. **Advertise with Us:** Calling on Christian and Conservative Businesses. We are also calling on Christian-owned and conservative businesses across the nation to partner with us by purchasing ad space in Capitol Times Magazine. In a world where mainstream media often shuns businesses that stand for faith and conservative principles, we offer you an audience that shares your values. When you advertise with us, you reach a community that respects traditional values, loves America, and seeks businesses that align with their beliefs.

We are offering special advertising packages for 2025 that allow businesses to connect directly with our growing readership. Whether you're promoting your company, service, or a conservative cause, Capitol Times Magazine provides the perfect platform to amplify your message. By advertising with us, you not only gain exposure but also help to keep conservative media alive and thriving in the face of opposition.

Why Advertise with Us?

Engaged Readership

- Our readers actively seek quality content, making your ads more likely to be noticed.

Multi-Platform Visibility

- Maximize your exposure through our print and digital platforms.

Cost-Effective Solutions

- Affordable packages designed to fit various budgets.

Contact Us

For inquiries and bookings, please contact our advertising team at ads@capitoltimesmedia.com

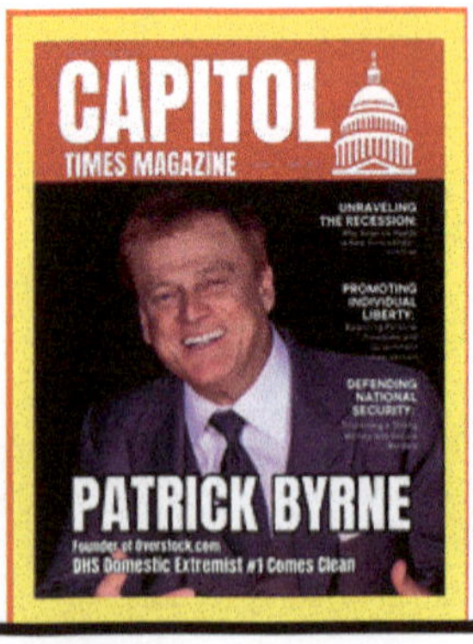

Join Us in Keeping the Faith

As conservatives, we know that this battle for the soul of America is not just political—it's spiritual. The cultural war being waged against the values of faith, family, and freedom can only be won with your support. As the Left pushes further toward socialism and radical agendas, Capitol Times Magazine remains committed to our guiding principles rooted in Christianity and conservatism.

Now, more than ever, our country needs strong, principled media outlets that stand unwaveringly for God, freedom, and country. Capitol Times Magazine is proud to be one of those voices, but we need your help to stay strong in the fight.

With your support, we can continue to shine a light on the issues that matter most and give a voice to the leaders and ideas that will preserve America's greatness. Together, we can protect our values, our country, and our future.

Support Capitol Times Magazine today. For truth. For freedom. For America.

JEWELZ
YOGA
For Every Body
Whether Beginner or
Advanced, Our
Classes Welcome All
Start Your Journey Now
www.jewelzyoga.com
Advertisement